Five Steps From Eternity

Lanae's Death—
A Family's Journey Through Grief

Leanne Paetkau

Cover Design by Randi Gammons:
randigammons@hotmail.com
Edited by Debra Sonnichsen:
multitasking_mama@yahoo.ca
Formatted by Amber Downey:
amber@fixerfairy.com

Foreword

Dear Friend,

This lovely book is about Lanae, a precious young woman whose life here was cut short—but-whose eternal life has just begun. *Five Steps From Eternity* draws you into the life of a mother grieving her loss, and the reflections of loved ones describing their own anguish. You will also read about the light of God's love and compassion, bringing comfort and hope to those in mourning.

I first met Leanne when she joined a course I was facilitating. Days after the course had finished, Leanne contacted me to say her daughter had just been killed in a backcountry ski accident. Months later Leanne invited me to help her write Lanae's story. Helping write this book has been an honour – a special but difficult assignment from God. Leanne and I spent several days in a beautiful cottage (thank you Diana) working on the book morning to night.

Five Steps From Eternity is based on Leanne's raw and emotional journal, born out of deep unimaginable grief. Leanne went from trusting God and being surrendered to His will, to wanting an answer to that unanswerable question "Why?" Grief is such a distressing roller-coaster ride—trusting one moment, doubting the next, then trusting again. It was heart-wrenching reading the journal with Leanne, asking for clarification on some of the entries, realising this would re-open wounds—yet knowing God was comforting her heart.

In the midst of this pain, God has brought a beacon of hope and light and joy to Leanne and her loved ones—a deepened trust and longing for Him. They have been crushed but not forsaken. It was a blessing to meet John, Logan, Alicia, and Daniel, and to see Lanae's life through their eyes. I know the prayers of God's people have bathed them all in peace that passes understanding. I am sure as you read this book you will be drawn to the love and faithfulness of God. We grieve but know we will see Lanae again … and so we rejoice!

Blessings,
Rena Groot

Dedication

This book is lovingly dedicated to my husband John.

Without his giant sized faith in the character of his Lord and Saviour Jesus, and God's Word, I would have surely caved in as our tragedy unfolded. He had such strong resilience in the face of so much loss and grief. It was also how he faced the events of February 24th, 2022, in Ukraine. We were already deeply grieving our place where we had hoped to return, to serve, plus the huge tragic losses our fellow brothers and sisters in Christ were facing in Ukraine. John has been and continues to be a mighty bulwark for me. After Jesus' great gospel for me, John is the next greatest gift that has ever been given to me.

"There was a man sent from God; His name was John." (John 1:6) This verse changed the course of our relationship.

All my love to you Honey,
Leanne

Special Thanks to:

My precious Jesus is first and foremost. He gave me life and gave our daughter the escape route to Heaven through His precious blood shed on the cross of Calvary, 2000 years ago, and through His empty grave.

I will forever praise Him and rejoice in Him for all that He has accomplished on my behalf.

The "Paetkau Tribe", Alicia and Garrett Jones, Daniel, and Logan Schroeder. Without all of you helping me to navigate these tumultuous waters, I wouldn't have had the balance that I needed.

Rena Groot, who travelled so far and sacrificed her time and energy to come alongside me and help me to get the book down on the computer. I am so grateful for her writing expertise and so graciously giving to me from the overflow of what Jesus has lavished on her. Thank you also to Rena for succinctly writing the foreword to my book.

Diana Witbeck, who blessed us with a beautiful hideaway as a peaceful place to write.

4

Chapter One

Departure Day: Lanae's Last Hurrah
April 13, 2022
Five Steps From Eternity....

These are Lanae's last footsteps…

Monday, August 15th, 2022
"So that you will not grieve (for them) as the others do who have no hope (beyond this present life)."

I desperately needed to know what happened—
not in my head—but in my heart. My head
logically told me that the cornice, an
outcropping of ice and snow that looks like part
of the mountain but isn't, let go.
I reasoned she must have hit her head hard, and
that she fell a long, long way. I knew
theologically, God would have been there
caring for her—helping her. But spiritually,
from God's point of view, what happened?
I sat on the edge of the Bow River in
Cochrane—thinking—praying—crying. I
needed to know more. I needed to know that
when we weren't there to catch our Sweetie,
my husband and I, Someone else was.
As I looked to the sky, with tears streaming, I
cried "LORD, God what happened?" I felt like
maybe I was too angry so perhaps I couldn't
hear Him—perhaps He had rejected me and
turned His back to me.
"She fell so far, God—almost the height of two
Calgary towers. How could she have fallen that
far and not been completely broken—
completely smashed? John and Logan saw her
in the morgue in Golden. She was completely
whole—not twisted and mush."

John said she looked as if she had taken a
bad fall from her mountain bike, and hit her
face hard.
Her Garmin watch measured everything. She
fell at 80 kilometres per hour.

"LORD! Were you there? Please, LORD, I need to know in my heart what happened and how you were there for her."

"Leanne, Leanne…" I heard God's quiet, not audible voice inside me.

"Lanae was on the cornice. The cornice let go. She fell. She hit her head on the outcropping of rock. She went unconscious. She left her body and could see herself falling." God told me about His conversation with my daughter. He is such a good Father.

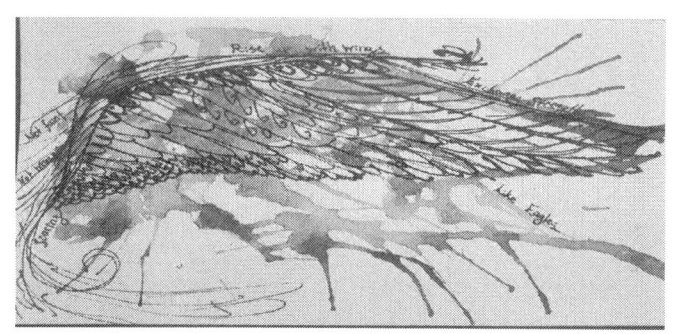
One of Lanae's hand-made cards

"Lanae, you can go back into your body, and it will be hard, but I will be with you…or you can come home with Me. Leanne, she chose to come home with me. So I told her, ``Okay, let me show you how to fly."

"But LORD, it was so far to fall. How LORD? How is it possible she's not completely broken?"

"Leanne, I carried her down. I was there to carry her."

I sobbed.

When John and I couldn't be there to catch our little girl, God was there, and caught her for us. The next day, a report from BC Parks was reported in Global News. It said a woman from Cochrane had fallen and Search & Rescue found her partially buried in the snow. But that wasn't what God said to me. I held my breath. "Lord?"

The next day, Global News had an update and a correction. The woman from Cochrane was found lying on top of the snow debris…not buried at all.

When I read the corrected update, I cried again. God was confirming and verifying His word to me—that He carried Lanae down that horrible drop and laid her gently on the top of the snow.

This is the last photo of Lanae. Looking at that photo I realise Lanae is a victor over death.
God broke the curse of death for me too.
The law of the Spirit of Life in Christ Jesus has set me free from the law of sin and death.
The grave is empty for Lanae—for me.
Here I am, Lord. Please bring healing.
My heart is so broken.
I need you to walk with me on this spinning potter's wheel.
I am confident that You, the Master Potter, are shaping a clay pot that will be beautiful and useful for You—however You see fit. I am Yours, Lord.
I surrender myself and all I have into Your loving hands.
I and the children You have given me are safe.
Lanae recorded a video on March 9th, 2021. She knew we would need to hear this message on May 9, 2022, Victory Day. Lanae referenced Psalm 116. God directed me to look it up. The title in my Amplified Bible is *Thanksgiving for Rescue from Death*. I already knew before I read the verses, that the Lord was going to teach me lessons He intended for this season of my life from this Scripture.

"*I love the LORD, because He hears (and continues to hear) my voice and my*

supplications (my pleas, my cries, my specific needs). Because He has inclined His ear to me, Therefore, I will call on Him as long as I live."
Psalm 116:1-2

I know Lanae called on Him when she fell. He was inclining His ear to her. He answered her.

The cords and sorrows of death encompassed me, And the terrors of Sheol came upon me; I found distress and sorrow.
Psalm 116:3

10

When the cords of death started entangling Lanae's feet and the terrors of Sheol came upon her…they came upon me as well. I knew something was wrong. Distress and sorrow found me…her mom.

Then I called, on the name of the LORD; O, LORD, please save my life!
Psalm 116:4

The LORD answered Lanae. Her soul was already safe with Him, secure in His safety deposit box. At three years old she said, "I sang Jesus into my heart, Mom", as she handed me her soother—relinquishing her precious soskah into my hand for good, telling Jesus He was now her comforter.

She gave her life to obey Him. At seven when she ran into an unjust authority at school, she chose to obey Jesus and show love. At fifteen she followed Jesus obediently into the river for baptism and surrendered her future, her goals and dreams into His hands. "My life is Yours, Lord Jesus."

anae's Baptism in Sumy, Ukraine – 2009

He saved her life—mine too. Although the cords of death wrapped around us—encircling. They couldn't hold us. Jesus threw them off.

Gracious is the Lord and (consistently) righteous. Yes, our God is compassionate. Psalm 116:5

The Lord Jesus carried her down the mountain and gently laid her to rest on her beloved white snow. The cornice, the wind-swept snow that overhung the edge of the mountain, did not overcome her. She was protected and safe.

12

The LORD protects the simple (childlike); I
was brought low (humbled and discouraged),
And He saved me.
Psalm 116:6

Lanae was always child-like.
The newspaper called her a woman. Yes, she was married, but she was so child-like and innocent—naïve in a way—so easily distraught about and hurt by the evil of this world.
I am sure she felt humbled as she fell. Did she think, I wasn't careful enough? Was she discouraged as the cornice broke away from the packed snow field and she began to fall? I know she was aware of her Saviour's Presence. I can hear her saying, "HE SAVED ME! JESUS IS MY HERO!"
One cannot be truly saved unless they become like a little child confident in the Saviour's love—humbled as they realise their great need for God in everything. We cannot even take our next breath without Him. Lanae was saved that day. She went safely home. The other skiers went away, lost. I pray that they will be found.

Return to your rest, O my soul,
For the LORD has dealt bountifully with you.
Psalm 116:7

I hear Jesus speaking to my heart,
Take My yoke upon you, Leanne, and learn from Me, (following Me as My disciple), for I am gentle and humble in heart, and you will find rest (renewal, blessed quiet) for your souls.
Matthew 11:29

I can rest because I know Lanae is at rest. I can trust Him with her. He is gentle and humble in heart.

For You have rescued my life from death, My eyes from tears, And my feet from stumbling and falling,
Psalm 116:8

This is Lanae's story. This story doesn't end on Mount Des Poilus. She was saved from death, her eyes from tears, and her feet—her footsteps—from falling. She didn't fall that day. Jesus swooped in, scooped her up, and away they flew. She lives forever. In fact, she is now more alive than we on Earth have ever been. She is home. Safe and sound. No more tears or sorrow or pain.

I will walk (in submissive wonder) before the
LORD in the land of the living.
Psalm 116:9

Help me, LORD, as Lanae's mom, to keep
walking in submissive surrender and wonder
before You in the land of the living.

I believed (and clung to my God) when I said,
"I am greatly afflicted."
Psalm 116:10

I feel greatly afflicted and conflicted right now.
My world has shifted. I am determined to cling
more and more to God—believing in Him, on
Him, and from Him—having faith in Him as
never before.

I said in my alarm, all men are liars.
Psalm 116:11

There was a deep pain in Lanae's heart that there are so many liars in the world. There is so much corruption and evil—it grieved her heart.

***What will I give to the LORD (in return) for all His benefits toward me? (How can I repay Him for His precious blessings?)
Psalm 116:12***

God blessed me so much having Lanae for twenty-seven and a half years. How can I ever thank Him enough for lending her to me?

***I will lift up the cup of salvation and call on the name of the LORD.
Psalm 116:13***

Yes, Lord, let me—let everyone, call on Your name. For there is no other name under Heaven by which we must be saved.

***I will pay my vows to the LORD, yes, in the presence of all His people.
Psalm 116:14***

What promises and vows did I make to the Lord? This event was untimely in my eyes, but God knows the end from the beginning. Lanae's early call home doesn't change any of my vows. My marriage would still be "to the

Praise of His Glorious Grace", my decision that I would be His bondservant and follow Christ with all my heart, that I was His alone—that I would seek His Kingdom and His Righteousness, and then all these things would be added to me—those vows are all intact. Nothing changed. My question remained. "What would you have me do now, Lord?"

Precious (and of great consequence) in the sight of the LORD, Is the death of his godly ones (so He watches over them).
Psalm 116:15

You mean, He watches over the details of the godly one's deaths? He cares even how, when, where, and what happens to them? His hand holds and orchestrates the events of our lives? He coordinates it? That's how precious it all is to him? (I'm yelling and screaming inside right now as I write this.)
Can I let her go for a while? She was precious—so precious to me. Now it's God's turn—her death is precious to Him. It's His turn, Leanne. Let go and let Him have His perfect way. He will always do what's best— what is pleasing and perfect and good.

Oh Lord, truly I am your servant, the son (daughter) of your handmaid; you have unfastened my chains.

Psalm 116: 16

Through my suffering, through my loss, perhaps you're setting me free. You have unfastened my chains—so although I am a bond servant, I am not a slave. I am free! I want to be useful to you in this time of suffering. I want to be 100% aware of how I am glued to you, and that you supremely love me. Here I am Lord. Send me.

I will offer to You, the sacrifice of Thanksgiving, and will call on the name of the Lord.
Psalm 116:17

Yes, now my thanks-givings will pour out of these pages. I am thankful and grateful for so much. I will grieve and call on His name. I will be grateful.

Friday, August 12th, 2022
Yesterday was my day of surrender.
I completely surrendered Lanae to the LORD—to what happened.
I gave my Sweetie back to the LORD.
I yielded and submitted to God all that took place.
I gave up fighting against reality.
Here I am, LORD—do with me as You wish.

I am not my own. I am Yours.

Take all of me. All that I am. All that I have.

All my dreams, desires, expectations. I surrender them to You.

I am not my own. I've been bought with a price.

Here I am LORD. I am Yours.

These verses are speaking to my heart.

" For I am convinced (and continue to be convinced—Beyond any doubt) that neither death nor life, neither angels nor principalities, Nor things present and threatening, nor things to come, nor powers, Nor height, nor depth, nor any other created thing, will be able to separate us from the (unlimited) love of God, which is in Christ Jesus our Lord."
Romans 8:38-39.

Shall we indeed accept (only) good from God and not (also) accept adversity and disaster?
Job 2:10b

April 16th, 2022

Lanae fell asleep in Christ. She is not lost. She will be raised from the dead with an incorruptible, beautiful, immortal body. In Christ all who have believed in Him, will be made alive at His coming.

Now we do not want you to be uninformed, believers, about those who are asleep, (in death), So that you will not grieve (for them) , as the others do who have no hope (beyond this present life), For if we believe that Jesus died and rose again (as in fact He did), even so God (In this same way—by raising them from the dead) will bring with Him those (believers) who have fallen asleep (in Jesus). For we say this to you by the Lord's (own)word, that we who are still alive and remain until the coming of the Lord, will in no way precede (into His presence) those (believers) who have fallen asleep (in death). For the Lord Himself will come down from heaven, with a shout of command, with the voice of the archangel and with the (blast of the) trumpet of God, and the dead in Christ will rise first. Then we who are alive and remain (on the earth) will simultaneously be caught up (raptured) together with them (the resurrected ones) in the clouds to meet the Lord in the air, And so we will always be with the Lord!

Therefore comfort and encourage one another with these words (concerning our reunion with believers who have died).
1 Thessalonians 4:13-18

Lanae put herself at risk and wasn't afraid of danger, because she believed in what God said—that there is a resurrection of our bodies. Sometimes it seemed she couldn't wait.

Me: "Why did You take her home on April 13th?"

God: "It was best for her, for all of you."

Me: "Why now?"

God: "Her project, the one I had given her to do, was completed here on earth. It was time to move onto the next assignment that I had for her. I needed her here."

Me: "Thank you Lord, You took Lanae home when You did, how You did—Your ways are best."

Nov 2021

Dear Mom,

Happy Birthday! Time & years don't matter compared to eternity — but I'm thankful for the yearly opportunity that your birthday is to say how thankful I am for you!

When I think about it, who you are in my life & what you have done for me, our family — & God — it makes me want to cry! (Good tears)

Thank you for your wisdom, grace, & patience towards all of us, me especially because I know that I have been a hard challenge for you.

Also you are an amazing Grandma & it brings me much joy to watch you with Liam!

My prayer for you: May God bless you spiritually & in your physical health — pouring out His grace upon grace, giving you renewed strength, joy, & much fruit + heavenly rewards as you continue to pour yourself out in service to Him! May your joy be multiplied greatly this year as you continue to step into this season of preparation for His coming.

♡ Laura

Chapter Two

Stepping into Joy

Resurrection Sunday, April 17th, 2022
Thank You, Lord, for your power which raised Christ from the dead. That same power dwells in me and in Lanae. You will raise up her body one day—sown a corruptible body—raised incorruptible—sown a mortal body—raised an immortal body.

April 18th, 2022
Lanae's been gone five days now. I am so sad... I miss my Sweetie. Thank you, Lord, for her life. She lived so fully, and so fully for You.

April 20th, 2022
I am still serving, loving, worshipping, crying, praising, waiting, breathing, crushed—but not without hope. Hope that sees its object with physical eyes, touch, taste, smell, hearing, is not true hope. For hope is not focused on what one has, but rather on the thing which it does not have. I cannot see right now, into the future glory that we will live in, but I know that that glory outweighs the pain, sadness and loss that I am experiencing right now. It will be worth it!!

And not only this, but we too, who have the first fruits of the Spirit [a joyful indication of the blessings to come], even we groan inwardly, as we wait eagerly for [the sign of] our adoption as sons—the redemption and transformation of our body [at the resurrection]. For in this hope we were saved [by faith]. But hope [the object of] which is seen is not hope. For who hopes for what he already sees?
Romans 8:24-25

I put my hope and my expectation into what I know is mine, even though, right now it is not in my hand, not in my scope of vision, and not familiar to my senses of touch and smell. I am there, where He—my Jesus is, and one day my body will catch up. My faith, my hope, my expectation will be sight—and will be realised in the truest of ways.

So then, being always filled with good courage and confident hope, and knowing that while we are at home in the body, we are absent from the Lord.
2 Corinthians 5:6

April 22nd, 2022
More than one week has gone by and my Sweetie is with Jesus and with our ABBA.

Wow! In the presence of God forever. No more suffering, crying, hunger, low blood sugars, grumpy, losing perspective, fighting against her body and the physical limitations of this broken world.

Help me Lord—I am struggling today.

Thank You, Lord, for the hymn promising You will take care of me. "No matter what may be the test, God will take care of you. Lean weary one, up-on His breast, God will take care of you."(Hymn Civilla D. Martin)

April 23rd, 2022
My heart aches at night—again in the morning—again at night. If only I could have twenty-four more hours to pour out my mother's love on my girl, on my Sweetie. Oh, for an hour to just hold her hand and hug her— to stroke her hair and look into her beautiful deep sky-blue eyes.
Thank You, Lord, for the gift of Lanae Katherine. Thank You that I got to hold her close for so many years.

April 25th, 2022
Two more days until the funeral that I am dreading…

Please be my help and strength oh Lord—in me, Lord—through me, Lord. I am seated with You Lord Jesus, in the Heavenly realms. Wednesday, April 27th, I'm going to tuck myself into You on Your lap all day long.

April 26th, 2022
Be still Leanne, and know that I am God.
I hung on to Your Word today, Lord, as I went to see Lanae's left-behind body.

S

umy, Ukraine

Wednesday, April 27th, 2022
This was the day of the celebration of Lanae's life. The service was held in the Alliance church in Cochrane Alberta. The internment was in the Cochrane cemetery.

She crowned You as Lord in life. You are her Lord in death. One beautiful day she will cast her crown before You in the eternal realm. Thank You for taking such good care of my Sweetie.

Jesus once spoke to a little girl asleep in death. "'Talitha Kum'! Little Girl, I say to you, arise." One day my Sweetie will rise. Then we will eat together in Your glorious Kingdom—together with all the church— Your body—Your bride. LORD, You are not the God of the dead, but of the living! Thank you for holding my Sweetie, taking such good care of her Lord while she walked this earth and as she stepped into eternity.

Such a glorious blue-sky day, with fluffy white clouds. What a beautiful day to lay my Sweetie to rest, to be sown into the ground—to be planted. Her pillow was the green/brown striped one from our living room, graced with a pillowcase, white with pink and green embroidered flowers. The pillowcases had been a gift from the missionary box of the E Free Church of Bow Island, Alberta. The pillow held her neck up in a normal sleeping position. What I loved the most though, were all the pine branches underneath her—the evergreen—with a splash of brown colour—as the baby pinecones surrounded her head. Her arms lay still on either side of her body, just as if she was asleep. Her fingers were curled up, resting in their sleeping positions, thumbs gracing the side, hugging the fingers as they curled under and nestled. Her thumb nail still looked ready to take on any task that required its short, sturdy length—like the untying and undoing of a knot. How I miss seeing her vivacious blue eyes that danced and smiled. The funeral director let me "Mom" her, gently smooth lotion on her hand. Her lips were not slightly apart, with the look of night sleeping, breathing quiet breath—rather they were tightly closed with no expression of pain or ache or pout on them—painted over with antique-rose coloured cream to hide the expected blue-lip colour of death. Her whole face was covered in a foundation of colour, unlike her own—hiding the blue tones that would have taken over her rose coloured cheeks. Her eyebrows were now defined— never before had they ever been painted on. Her hair had a spot of colour—the bright orange, silky, flower clip—that she had always loved to wear, pulling her hair back. Her bangs were brushed gently to the side of her forehead, her lashes black and full.

The side of her face and her eye had been swollen, John had told me. Now there was absolutely no swelling—it was gone. She looked so peaceful.

Her right arm at the wrist showed some trauma—it was so blue and bruised—swollen— wrapped in gauze I guess to hold it together.

This was the only visible injury that I could see on her. Lanae had never ever broken a limb or even sprained an ankle in all of her running, soccer playing, climbing trees, horse-back riding, jumping, skiing, and climbing mountains.

Her beautiful feet that always ran everywhere they went, were also in their resting positions— toes slightly pointing in towards each other. Her legs—so solid and hard—so athletic looking— were now cold, frozen, not soft, not ready to rise up and run.

They were so still—so quiet—I have never seen her lay so still—not a twitch—not a muscle moving.

I gave the funeral home a bra to put on her, one I had bought just for her at the store. Her sports bras would not have worked with her beautiful blouse.

It helped to fill in her chest, under her royal blue blouse, with the tassels and embroidered colours of orange, yellow, white and red. She looked so beautiful to me, in her blue *vyshyvanka blouse—and black flared yoga pants, and cute blue 'bright-with-flowers' socks.

*Ukrainian embroidered blouse

She liked cute socks.

How could it be Lord, that she was not all twisted and crushed, laying there at an odd angle? Or that her neck was not all crooked? Hadn't she fallen so far down that mountain? How can this be Lord?
How can this literally be possible?
I was seeing my Sweetie in death, and yet she was still so beautiful. Later, we as a family lay beautiful sunflowers on her as she lay in her casket. I wanted to, but didn't dare say it out loud: "Wake up, Lanae! Wake up! Time to wake up!"—for fear that decreeing it verbally, she would suddenly hear from the other world, and come back. How could I wish her back?

Instead, I chose to say:
> "Lanae—I am so proud of you!
> You did well, Sweetie.
> You lived life so well.
> Have a good sleep, Lanae. I love you.
> See you in the morning."

April 30th, 2022
We will never go through an April ever again, where it will feel normal, familiar. Instead, our lives have changed forever. We waited two long weeks to have closure—till April 27th, due to the bureaucracy of an autopsy and out of province death.
Finally, the day of closing the lid came, buckling the leather straps tight. She is asleep in the dust of the earth, but one day, will awaken to a new fresh start…

> *...and the dead in Christ will rise first.*
> *After that, we who are still alive and are left*
> *will be caught up*
> *together with them in the clouds to meet the*
> *Lord in the air.*
> *And so we will be with the Lord forever.*
> *Therefore encourage one another with these*
> *words."*
> *1 Thessalonians 4:16b-18*

May 2nd, 2022

I, Leanne Paetkau, feel God is taking me to a new chapter. I am calling it Voskreseneeyeh—Resurrection in Russian. He is the restorer of LIFE. Generations ago, God restored a lost lineage of family to Ruth and Naomi.

May he also be to you one who restores life and sustains your old age; for your daughter-in-law, who loves you and is better to you than seven sons, has given birth to him."
Ruth 4:15

Why are you troubled, and why do doubts arise in your heart?
Luke 24:38

Leanne? Why are you troubled? Why do doubts arise in your heart? BELIEVE!" Jesus says to me…

Jesus said to her, "I am the Resurrection and the Life. Whoever believes in (adheres to, trusts in, relies on) Me [as Saviour] will live even if he dies; and everyone who lives and believes in Me [as Saviour] will never die. Do you believe this?"
John 11:25-26

"The LORD gave and the LORD has taken away; Blessed be the name of the LORD."
Job 1:21b

O
ne of Lanae's handmade cards

May 4th, 2022
Thank You, Lord! Your coming is soon!
Thank You that we have Your Word!
Your Word is sure and certain.

"For yet in a very little while, he who is coming will not delay."
Hebrews 10:37

"So that the one who reads it (the vision) will run. For the vision is yet for the appointed time; It hastens towards the goal and it will not fail. Though it tarries wait for it; For it will certainly come, it will not delay."
Habakkuk 2:2b-3

34

This is the vision that Lanae had! It was given to the one who reads it, so that the one who reads it would feel confident to run, to take risks. Lanae ran, Lord, You know how she ran! That's why she was not afraid to run! She had the vision!!

May 19th, 2022
Would Lanae have been horrified by her own death? Yes, she probably would have reacted the worst of all of us. She would've been devastated by losing a loved one in the way that we lost her. Somehow, it's comforting knowing this, that God spared her the ordeal—the learning curve we are all on. God was good to take her home when He saw it was best—to take her in a way that brought the most glory to Himself. God reassured me today. He fulfilled this verse in Lanae's life.

> *The steps of a (good and righteous) man are directed and established by the Lord, and He delights in his way and blesses his path. When he falls, he will not be hurled down, because the Lord is the one who holds his hand and sustains him.*
> *Psalm 37: 23-24*

God literally directed her footsteps that day. He steered her in the direction He wanted her to go. It was never a matter of, would He not allow her to fall, but that when she did fall, she wouldn't be hurled down and then crushed and torn apart. The Lord was with her, therefore, He held and sustained her.

Lord thank you, that You are holding me and bearing my burden. I could not carry it one more step. I surrendered—You grabbed my burden—taking it for me. I gave it all to You. I don't have to have an emotional response to it all anymore. You are surrounding me with love rather than the burden—filling me with Your love rather than me carrying, crying and dealing with the pain. I see You Jesus, holding me. I finally can release all the pain, all the fear, all the helplessness.

May 20th, 2022

I will give a sacrifice of praise—even though I hurt—am dismayed—I will praise You and give You thanks. You had a reason—A BIG IMPORTANT ONE—to take Lanae home. Even though I feel shocked—beyond that—broken—I will trust in YOU! I WILL SURRENDER!

"For no heart can conceive in what surpassing love God giveth us this myrrh; yet this which we are to receive to our souls good, we suffer to pass by us in our sleepy indifference, and nothing comes of it." (Streams In The Desert, May 20)

I feel God speaking to me often. He is carrying me.

I know that my Redeemer liveth,
and on the earth again shall stand;
I know eternal life He giveth,
that grace and power are in His hand.
I know His promise never faileth,
The word He speaks, it cannot die.
Though cruel death my flesh assaileth,
yet I shall see Him by and by.
I know my mansion He prepared,
That where He is there I may be;
Oh wondrous thot, for me He careth,
And He at last will come for me.
I know, I know that Jesus liveth,
And on the earth again shall stand,
I know that life He giveth,
That grace and power are in His hand.
Based on Job 19:25
(Hymn by Pounds and Fillmore)

"Beware, Leanne, that you don't have a sleepy indifference to the myrrh that has been given to you." I know it is to my soul's good that I receive it.

"Help me Lord, to receive your gift of myrrh, in the right spirit."

May 21st, 2022
He works on me to make me more fragrant. May I be a pleasing aroma to those who are His—those looking for Him—those looking for life and life more abundantly.

Lord, take the emptiness of my heart and fill it with you!

I cannot and will not stay in this pit of despair and despondency any longer.
Enough is enough!
My Lanae is at home with Jesus.
We put her on the train and she has arrived. She is waiting for us.
She is where she should be—right on time—no questions need to be asked. My human side has many questions, I so much want to understand why—but I fully yield it all now to my Captain. He has shown Himself trustworthy in the past and so I will 100% surrender all my doubts, my questions, and my pain to Him now. I ask Him for a fresh start—a chance to get back in the game—to know He will continue to heal my

aching heart. He will continue to mend me, comfort me, hug me, and He will use this unexpected turn of events for His glory and honour.

For we know that if the earthly tent (our physical body) which is our house is torn down (through death)—and this is the reality for Lanae—for now her earthly body is out of commission—her house has been set aside—but God values her house dearly.

"For we know that if the earthly tent [our physical body] which is our house is torn down [through death], we have a building from God, a house not made with hands, eternal in the heavens. For indeed in this house we groan, longing to be clothed with our [immortal, eternal] celestial dwelling, so that by putting it on we will not be found naked. For while we are in this tent, we groan, being burdened [often weighed down, oppressed], not that we want to be unclothed [separated by death from the body], but to be clothed, so that what is mortal [the body] will be swallowed up by life [after the resurrection]. Now He who has made us and prepared us for the very purpose is God…"
2 Corinthians 5:1-5a

Lanae is clothed right now—she's not just a spirit floating around. If I tell you I saw her in a vision you might think I'm crazy. But I'm not and I did. She looked more alive than I have ever seen her. She was peeking out from behind Jesus' shoulder. Her hair was long and curly. Her dress was flowing—brilliant red with yellow flowers. She had a beaming smile on her face—so full of joy. I was stunned. I was talking to Jesus, hoping to hear His reassuring voice, when He allowed me to see her. I felt like He held back the curtain so I could see her for a moment. He could have just said—Trust Me. She's safe here—but He gave me a glimpse behind the veil to see my precious daughter.

She was created for this very purpose. To be born a mortal, a human being—then her mortal body would one day be SWALLOWED UP BY LIFE (after the Resurrection). Yes! This is her purpose—God's purpose for her—to have lived, groaned, been burdened—put into a position of dependency on God for LIFE! Her daily bread! – then to go through separation— separated from her body—so resurrection life will swallow up her mortal body.

May 22nd, 2022

Lanae was willing to yield—she was being wise, but was still directed by God to go—and so she went. I can praise God—and thank Him—that she went—that she packed her gear on Monday, April 11th and left early Tuesday, April 12th. She went…

Thank You, Lord. This was the hardest sacrifice of praise ever for me—to praise You—that even in her going on the trip—and in her death—You are good. I trust that You did what was best for Lanae, for the other skiers, for Logan, for me, for John, for Alicia, for Daniel, for Garrett, for Liam, for Jaclyn, and for all of Lanea's friends, co-workers and colleagues.

You did the very best, God…

ogan, Lanae, and their Freedom 8848 hiking
buddies

May 25th, 2022

I have the realization that Lanae chose her path,
and I don't need to "own" it, or suffer her
consequences. They are her consequences—not
mine. I know this sounds really harsh, but
unless I separate myself from her, I will not
survive. John needs me, Alicia and Liam, baby
Jones and Garrett too. I need to be present, to
be engaged mentally, not to be checked out
with grief. Lanae's death is not my cross to
bear.

There—I said it.

I need to be here for Daniel—for his day-to-day need for a listening ear—for the mother's hug when he comes home in June. I want to look forward to his homecoming rather than feeling numb at the thought of him coming, not knowing how I am going to cope. When my dad died, John said he lost me for a year. I have to rise above this grief. I want to be here for the reasons God has me here—to thrive, to live. For me to live is Christ—to be on mission with Him—to love and enjoy Him! There—I have written it out in black-and-white and now I can put action steps to my desire and decision to be free.

Thank You, Lord!!

I used to think, to believe, that if I got all the wrinkles and lumps out of my "bed", my life, then I could lay down in peace and safety. No more— no—not now. God makes me lay down in those green pastures— the ones Jesus promised to me. He is in the business of restoring my soul.

My voice rises to God, and I will cry aloud; My voice rises to God, and He will hear me. In the day of my trouble I [desperately] sought the Lord; In the night my hand was stretched out [in prayer] without weariness; My soul refused to be comforted. I remember God; then I am disquieted and I groan; I sigh [in prayer], and my spirit grows faint. Selah.
Psalm 77:1-3

I have been groaning for days—the grief finally spilling over with unprompted tears. The Holy Spirit's voice has been interceding for me. I praise the Lord for the paraclete, the come along-sider, the Comforter. I have been unable to sleep deeply—dreading the darkness. It wants to envelop me. I dread and am filled with fear. I am drawn from room to room in my house as if in a dream—carrying my locked-up grief—sobs barely escaping. My soul is refusing the Lord's comfort. I feel like grief is swallowing me up.

There is a verse that says, "Blessed are those who mourn."

I do not feel blessed.

God, how does this make any sense? I am trusting You for the blessing to come—waiting on You. I don't see it—but if Your Word says it then it must be true.

I have been growing faint. My sighs seem unproductive.

I am reminded that Job wondered why he was even born. He had no hope of anything making a difference in his situation. His wife advised him to curse God and die. His friends felt there had to be secret sin in his life. Job finally recognized that God's ways cannot be understood or even questioned. He is God—and I am not. This has been a very difficult walk, Lord.

The last photo on Lanae's phone was taken forty minutes before her home-going.

How beautiful and delightful on the mountains
Are the feet of him who brings good news,
Who announces peace,
Who brings good news of good [things],
Who announces salvation,
Who says to Zion, "Your God reigns!"
Isaiah 52:7

Chapter Three
Yes Lord!

May 26th, 2022

Has it really, truly, already been six weeks since you went home? I still look for you every day. I listen for your running footsteps, and pause, hold my breath, but you're not there. You're there in Heaven with Jesus, and yet, in a way, you are laying in the field beside Big Hill. I know as a fact Lanae sees the face of Jesus, but until Resurrection Day, I'm not sure I one hundred percent get it. Lanae is with Jesus, but not yet in her resurrection body. I will trust the Lord with the "now but not yet" dimension. She is not just an ethereal spirit floating around. She has a body— she just doesn't have her beautiful, eternal body for now.

May 31ˢᵗ, 2022

I have some rhetorical questions today. I feel rejected, Lord. Will I feel rejected forever? You've been so favourable to me— Will You never answer my prayers again? I knew Your lovingkindness—has that ceased now? There were so many promises and Words from Your Living Word, Lord, that You gave to me regarding Lanae and Logan. How will they be fulfilled now? You were doing such amazing things through those two—have the blessings ended? And just like that—the wall of death came crashing down? You were always so gracious—have You forgotten to be gracious? Your compassion was so abundant—have You in Your anger withdrawn Your love for me, for them and others? I know the truth in my head, that the right hand of the most High has not changed. Your loving kindness has not been withheld.

> ***For I am convinced (and continue to be convinced beyond any doubt) that neither death nor life, nor angels, nor principalities, nor things present and threatening, nor things to come, nor powers, nor height, nor depth, nor any other created thing, Will be able to separate us from the unlimited love of God which is in Christ Jesus our Lord.***
> ***Romans 8:38-39***

God continues to be the same today as He was yesterday. He reminded me as I prayed, "Leanne, I am able. I do all things well. There is a whole future ahead for my WORD to be fulfilled. I will continue to use Lanae and Logan in the future. The BEST IS YET TO COME!"

Yes, LORD; be to me and to them, all that You have planned, and all that You have spoken. You are good, You are LOVE and NOTHING is too difficult for You. You have a whole future of AMEN, and SO BE IT. You will keep your WORD to me and fulfill all of Your promises. You are MORE than ABLE. Your word, ALL of it—

WILL BE FULFILLED.

Lanae loved riding horses – she learned in
Ukraine and continued in Canada

Last night Logan was at youth group, and brought home a gift made by one of the youth—a beautiful wooden, handmade coaster engraved with a burnt etching of the mountains and the words from Isaiah 52:7…

How beautiful and delightful on the mountains are the feet of him who brings good news, who announces peace, who brings good news of good (things,) who announces salvation, who says to Zion, "Your God reigns!".

Yes, Lanae's feet were beautiful. She was always in the mountains, proclaiming news of happiness to those who would listen.

June 2nd, 2022
Lord, I pray for strength to endure my loss and my great sadness here on this earth. I pray that when I am afraid (which I was this morning) I will trust in You. When I picture Lanae's purple Colts hoodie with the hole where the rock must have punctured her head—I will trust in You. Thank you for being there. You held her—and gently carried her down to her snowy bed. Thank You that You didn't allow her to be hurled down. Thank You that You supported her—even gave her a choice—she could choose to stay in her body in this world—or go home

with You. Thank You for Your tender Father love for my Sweetie.

anae and Logan on one of their adventures

June 3rd, 2022
Trust in the Lord with all your heart. Yes, Lord, it's time to trust You—not with part—but with all my heart. It's time to let, yield, surrender to Your powerful Holy Spirit—to allow Him to lead me on from here. Here is my stake in the sand. From here on, I look up and forward to what God is doing—in people's hearts and minds and bodies. He is Lord of all! He reigns! He is Sovereign! He knows what He's doing!

He cares about all His subjects involved in this drama. He works on behalf of all who love Him. He wraps His loving arms around us—holding us together so we don't fall apart –and He has us tucked into His loving Father's heart. All the answers to our questions are waiting for us. He is my God-Dad. I rest in Him.

June 4th, 2022
How far I've already come in my grief process…
1. I know Lanae's life was coming to some kind of impasse—there was a feeling that she couldn't keep going on this way. Something had to give. Something big had to change. I feel bad that I didn't speak words of warning—but would they have sounded silly? Would they have changed anything?
2. I know Lanae was thankful. I mentioned this before—but oh how I longed for a "note" from her, that she would have left behind. God directed me today to her Instagram account, and there I found my "note"! Lanae had recorded a video expressing her gratitude to her dad, Logan and I—for believing in her, and for giving her freedom to fly. *please watch her video. Go to thepaetkaus.net/thanks-logan-dad-mom-for/
3. What was still lacking that I needed to know? God's plans for me are good. Lord, speak please. I am listening. I feel like You are

saying, "Praise Me in the storm, Leanne". When I praise You, I see who You really are. I guess I believed and trusted You, God—for a miracle. This girl—me, this woman—came from poverty, from lack, from destruction, disappointment and despair. We were a ministry family derailed—my childhood family. My heart ached for years. I trusted God for rebuilding and restoration.

So… the miracle moment came… I got pregnant against all odds. We overcame—John and I. Our beautiful, darling baby girl was born. We gave her to Jesus—all of her—all of her life—inside the womb –her infant life—all of the facing-death moments with her. We surrendered her gladly. She was our sunbeam—but not ours to keep. We surrendered and offered and gave her back to God—asking that she would be a light in this dark world.

I have asked You Lord, that You will bring many lives to know Jesus, through this tragedy. My heart cries out "Lord, what's in it for me? I feel so selfish."

Can I even expect an answer? "I stand before You God, as Job stood before You. You are God and I am not. I was not there when you laid the foundations of the earth. I don't know how the goats give birth unaided on the edge of the mountain, or how the constellations remain suspended in the heavens on their own."

So, the questions for me are—the gift of Lanae for twenty-seven years and six months—as her mom—am I grateful for what I had with her? How many years would have been enough? Do I welcome Lanae's five steps from eternity? Do I have peace? Am I willing to say, YES, LORD. ANYWHERE. ANYTIME. ANYTHING. HERE I AM…TAKE HER.

These questions make me cry—hard, sobbing tears streaming down my face. When will my grief subside? Am I willing to say, "Have it all Lord—have it Your way—not my will be done but Yours."

I disagreed with Lanae's decision to go that day. I begged her to change her mind. We had no idea her payment of $150 to join the expedition was really payment for the opportunity to be a witness to the world—but, especially to four skiers—and to one in particular.

We had no idea this one decision to join this ski trip would send her off into the next chapter of her life. How I wish I could've said goodbye. One more hug—one more 'I am so delighted in you'—one more word of gratitude spoken to my daughter that I love.

Sunday, June 5th, 2022
I continue to grieve, but now my focus is up, outwards, and onwards.
What's next, Lord?
Heaven is literally around the corner. I am also going there. What a day of rejoicing that will be. My example is:

...Jesus, who is the Author and Perfecter of faith (the first incentive for our belief and the One who brings our faith to maturity), who for the joy (of accomplishing the goal) set before Him endured the cross, disregarding the shame, and sat down at the right hand of the throne of God (revealing His deity, His authority, and the completion of His work).
Hebrews 12:2

I have a cross to bear now.
But God has already gone before me and carried it all the way. I walk this path with Him, and I feel the pain He felt now.

But more than that, I count everything as loss compared to the priceless privilege and supreme advantage of knowing Christ Jesus my Lord (and of growing more deeply and thoroughly acquainted with Him—a joy unequaled). For His sake I have lost everything, and I consider it all garbage, so that I may gain Christ,
Philippians 3:8

I feel like many things in my life have been lost. Lanae is one of the many things… but, if I gain more knowledge of who Christ is, as He pertains to me, it's all worth it. He is worth more to me than anything I have or have had.
Please—just give me Jesus.

… and may be found in Him [believing and relying on Him], not having any righteousness of my own derived from [my obedience to] the Law and its rituals, but [possessing] that [genuine righteousness] which comes through faith in Christ, the righteousness which comes from God on the basis of faith.
Philippians 3:8-9

When He looks at me—into my heart—may He see only the reflection of His own righteousness that He placed there. When Jesus took my sin nature and put it onto Himself, He took my sin and in exchange gave me His very life, and in essence, all of His holiness, righteousness, and purity.

And this, so that I may know Him [experientially, becoming more thoroughly acquainted with Him, understanding the remarkable wonders of His Person more completely] and [in that same way experience] the power of His resurrection (which overflows and is active in believers], and [that I may share] the fellowship of His sufferings, by being continually conformed [inwardly into His likeness even) to His death [dying as He did]; Philippians 3:10

I am learning that I need to walk backwards in time to the point of Christ's resurrection—to the empty tomb. His body was not just gone—He arose from the dead. Now in His glorified body, He walked away—the first born from the dead. He conformed to death—knowing I died with Him in every way. His death was my death. He suffered greatly in my place. He understands. He went through this first—for me—for you.

I can let it be what He says it is—a "now but not yet". He is the first fruits of resurrection. Jesus died physically and was separated from God spiritually—He tasted death for all of us—therefore, physical death—

as someone who belongs to Christ, is simply an absence from the body—a clear and true presence with the Lord—the God of all life— the creator and sustainer of all that is.

Lanae is not in the grave, she is with Jesus—standing, running, talking, laughing— enjoying every moment with Him.

SHE IS HOME!

We will catch up—and soon be where she is—with the Lord forever. Her body will wake up out of its temporary sleep and we will all be quickened, changed, transformed with her—in the twinkling of an eye. Death will be swallowed up by immortality. The corruptible will overcome the incorruptible. SHE IS THERE NOW—but her body remains on earth—waiting to one day be renewed.

***...so that I may attain to the resurrection [that will raise me] from the dead.
Philippians 3:11***

The best for her—and for me—and for you—is yet to come. This is what Lanae has already attained spiritually—but one magnificent morning—will soon be attained physically for Lanae as well, and for all of us who remain on Earth. For me—and for you— there is fruitful labour. I look for those opportunities to be His mouth, His hands, His feet. I want to hear...

Well done, good and faithful servant.
Enter into the joy of Your Lord.
Matthew 25:23

June 8ᵗʰ, 2022

It is the eighth week of her departure. How I want to see her beaming smile and sparkling eyes. How I long to say, "Hi Lanae! I miss you so much!" –and just hear her voice saying, "Oh, hi Mom. I'm good. How are you?" I will savour that moment, and savour that interaction for the time to come—when finally, time will cease to be. Time is such a linear thing to be conquered one day. Once a man named Simeon waited to see the promised Messiah...

Simeon blessed them (Mary and Joseph) and said to Mary His mother,
Listen carefully:
this Child is appointed and destined for the fall and rise of many in Israel, and for a sign that is to be opposed—
and a sword [of deep sorrow] will pierce through your own soul—
so that the thoughts of many hearts may be revealed.
Luke 2:34-35

Mary had a prophecy that one day a sword of deep sorrow would pierce her soul—her heart—her life—her very being. The prophecy came true—the day Jesus Christ was mocked, ridiculed, abused, bullied, broken, tortured, and nailed to a wooden cross.

He took our place—the place of all adulterers, thieves, murderers, blasphemers—all who hate God and love evil. How Mary's heart must have trembled, as she realised that it must be so—and that she—no matter how she responded and was favoured of God—would have such pain one day. When that day came, she must have felt anguish watching her firstborn son abused, treated like a common criminal—when she knew He had done nothing wrong.

Did she know her precious son had to die so that many could live?

She knew from the prophecy, the thoughts of many hearts would be revealed. Mary would understand what I am going through. She would know the anguish of losing a child. It is comforting to know that.

What do Jesus' words of life mean to you? His giving of His flesh and blood for you—as our rescuer, redeemer, and restorer—a fixer of our problems that we have often brought upon ourselves—what does this cause you to see about yourself? What does He—the living, all-seeing God—the One who died for you—want to reveal to you about your own heart?

June 9th, 2022

Even on that day, April 13th, in Yoho National Park, You were there, God. No mountain Lanae could climb was too high for You. Your faithfulness towards her extended way beyond the clouds.

A question has been circulating, swirling, quietly percolating in my brain—what were Lanae's last thoughts—the last cries of her heart? I realised something—the thought was inching forward into my consciousness and is now in the front part of my mind. I believe Lanae's thoughts went beyond that moment—the moment she fell into Jesus' arms and landed in eternity. When she was swept away with her Lord, did her thoughts have many exclamation marks? Her thoughts must have been ones of wonder and delight and truly "out of this world". Thank you for wrapping Your arms around my Sweetie and faithfully seeing her across the great divide from time into eternity. You are so faithful. You have never failed me. Here I am Lord… send me. Send me to the countless readers who will observe and witness my sacrifice of praise to the One who loved me and gave Himself for me. YES LORD! YES LORD! YES LORD! Here I am—there she is—my special, unusual sunbeam of light—my daughter—my Sweetie. She is not mine to keep—not in life—not in death. She is all Yours. May Your will be done.

He is no fool who gives what he cannot keep
to gain what he cannot lose.
–Jim Elliot

Your lovingkindness and graciousness, O Lord, extend to the skies,
Your faithfulness [reaches] to the clouds.
Psalm 36:5

Chapter Four

Choosing Forgiveness

June 10th, 2022

Today, my soul refuses to be comforted. Why, Lord?

I should trust. I should not let my heart be troubled. I should be comforted by your Spirit—but God, everywhere I turn I see her. I see her friends, I see her trail running shoes, I hear her voice in her sister's voice, I see her nephew that never got to know his auntie, I see her baby chair with "Lanae" painted on it. I see her coat hanging—lifeless. I see her rollerblades—abandoned. I see her stuffy— Aunt Laurie's gift of a bunny—waiting for her on her pillow. I see her socks—the hockey socks worn over leggings when it was cold outside—crumpled on the floor where she hurriedly took them off Monday night. I see her notes to herself—what to pack, what to take, and off she went with no more entries written in her journal.

For all we know—as the ones who are left behind—she could have walked out that door, Tuesday at 3 AM, and been hit by a truck as she got into her vehicle to leave. Life is risky. There are no guarantees. Tomorrow is not promised to us. The evidence that has been left tells me this was no ordinary accident. I mean—her clothes were cut at the zippers—sheared off to release her from the cocoon of unnecessary material. Her beautiful Colts hoodie with Lanea embroidered on the sleeve—she was so proud of completing the Colts training as a purple decorated Colt—is folded up in the Funeral Home bag. Her orange signature winter coat—cut—her warmish, flexible, endurable pants—did exactly that—endure. Not a rip on them. Her socks? Her underwear? Her leggings? Where are they? Were they thrown into a bin at the morgue in Golden? How did she keep her legs warm? She never dressed warm enough. It was -25 that day. (Oh, the thoughts of a mother for her Sweetie.) Her black zippered warm-up jacket is there in the bag. Her green goggles are there. Her helmet is cracked. Her gloves? Missing. Her poles? Missing. Her ski boots—also signature orange to match her short alpine skis— missing one of the plastic protective tongues—were also in the bag. I see the drama displayed. One loonie sized ripped hole on the right side of her hoodie. The hoodie was over her helmet to give her warmth. She had her purple hood visible in her "take-off" photo. My Sweetie. Her beautiful blonde head was bruised by the mountain. I want to kiss you better. I want to hold you.

I want to sing to you once again, "A sunbeam, a sunbeam, Jesus wants you for a sunbeam. A sunbeam, a sunbeam, you'll be a sunbeam for Him."

You were a sunbeam, my Sweetie.

I would love to hold those calloused—not soft—hands in mine and pray together once more—interceding for our neighbours as we always did, your friends, your fears, your worries and longings—casting all of our cares before the Lord interceding and asking Him to carry them—trusting Him to answer them in His time.

I love you Lanae—so much—even though there was sickness—mental health issues. There were times you rejected me—took me for granted – fought against me—didn't listen—did not respect my space and my belongings. You gave us as parents all kinds of opportunities to be challenged by your strong will, to be hurt by your self-protective outer shell, to be put aside as you strove to make your way in your adult world. You learned at a snail's pace—to rest in His unchanging grace and love for you. You unknowingly pushed us away at times. Despite these hard times—and through it all—we loved you so much.

I often told you Lanae, that I loved you so much I would be willing to die for you—to give up my life for you——and yet there you went. You died anyway—without the opportunity for dad or I or Logan to lay our lives down for you—which we would have done in a heartbeat.

Sunday, June 12th, 2022

I cried for almost two hours on Saturday—journaling—and cried some more. Saturday night was incredible. I went to a ladies meeting for Mountain Springs Calvary Chapel, and there, to my surprise, were three special guests from Ukraine. I spoke a lot of Russian—and shared my heartache—translated for them—laughed with them—shared my Ukrainian chocolates with them. They had only been in Canada for four days. It was a God appointment. I moved on in my grief a wee bit. John helped me even more on Sunday.

> Lord, I surrender.
> Again.
> I give Lanae back to You.

Monday, June 13th, 2022

I thought I surrendered Lanae, all the different aspects of her, to the Lord. I have not. I am still holding her. It's time—I need to surrender her—her body—to accept that it's okay that she is laying in that grave.

I surrender her hands. They tied and untied so many knots—teaching others how to secure a safety rope.

I surrender her feet. They went all over the world—sharing the gospel—in Egypt, Jordan, Israel, Georgia, Canada, and especially Ukraine.

I surrender her marriage to Logan. He was hers for a while—but now they are both free of their marriage vows.

I surrender the past. The memories—both joyful and sorrowful—the hard times and the good.

I surrender her future possibilities. Future friends and companions she could have loved, taught, mentored.

I surrender her potential motherhood—all the flowers, Mother's Day cards, homemade gifts, laughter and giggles, gobbling up toes after bath time.

I surrender everything.

I surrender all of her youth group kids, her homeschooled wilderness survival kids that she was teaching, her clients for health-coaching, all whom she loved and whom she discipled—all of her great friends in Ukraine—and her MK friends scattered around the world—I surrender them all.

She loved them well to the end.

Thursday, June 16th, 2022

Yesterday as I walked to work, God and I had a detailed conversation. I will try to recall how it went.   "God, how is Lanae?

Why, God? What was your purpose in taking her home to Yourself in April?"

"It was a direct answer to your prayer, Leanne. You sensed that she wasn't heading in a good direction, and you cried out to Me, and I answered. She went early—compared to others her age—but right on time. I took her home before the enemy could sift her even further and her testimony—tarnished."

"Thank you, Lord. Thank you for guarding her and protecting her."

The righteous man perishes (at the hand of evil), and no
one takes it to heart; Faithful and devout men are taken
away, while no one understands that the righteous person
is taken away (to be spared) from disaster and evil.
Isaiah 57:1

June 17th, 2022

Thank you, Lord, that you have so many precious ones in your hands.

The man who lost his beloved wife— and now there is a widower and three motherless children.

The woman who has a precious baby in her womb—whom they want to birth prematurely, so that she can continue with cancer treatments. Oh Lord! Please bless and strengthen her. Help! All the details are in Your hands. Bring her baby girl safely into the world and bring complete healing to the mom.

Please strengthen me. Help me.

Support me this morning.

Please…

June 18th, 2022

All I can do in my moments of grief is to sit and hold my hands out to You, Lord—palms facing the sky. I know You have something for me to receive—and I want to be ready for it. I want my tears wiped away.

How can I get what You want for me, without first letting go of what cannot be mine?

How do I let go of all my hopes, dreams, expectations? Help me. Here you go, Lord.

June 19th, 2022

Mary cried out— Where have they laid Him? She longed to see her Rabbi, her Friend, her Teacher—just once more.

How I long to hear Lanae's voice—to have a hug from her. How I love her! How I miss her!

I receive by faith in You, Lord, that she is with You in paradise. She will not return here and now. But one day, I will go to her—and the biggest, longest hug is coming. I can imagine her saying…

"Mom, here's your hug. It's the sunshine on your shoulders. I love you."

"See you later, my Sunshine."

June 20th, 2022

Lord, help me today—energise me—strengthen my body.

Thank You, Lord, that You have a plan. You don't waste anything. Everything is in Your hands. Thank You that Your timing, Your grace, Your truth is being proclaimed through Lanae's death.

You gave Yourself—Your greatest gift—Your greatest sacrifice—to all of us—for all of us.

For God so [greatly] loved and dearly prized the world, that He [even] gave His [One and] only begotten Son, so that whoever believes and trusts in Him [as Savior] shall not perish, but have eternal life.
John 3:16

Then You, Father, got Him back, Your Son, Your beloved Son, in whom you were delighted and well pleased. John and I will get Lanae back—our daughter—our beloved—the one in whom we are delighted. We too will have fellowship with her once again.

June 25th, 2022

One day closer to our face-to-face encounter— the hug of all epic hugs—with Jesus, our best friend. I long for you, Jesus. I can't wait to see you with my own eyes. I am so glad to be going HOME!

There is a spot in my heart that refuses to be comforted—that refuses to receive the news— that resists acceptance.

Accept this? THIS?

I can't. I refuse to accept death.

End of discussion.

What I will accept is that death is not final. Lanae has gone away on a trip—for awhile—and is coming back—returning soon. I imagine hearing her say:
"I will return. I am not gone forever. I am more alive than ever before!!"

Lanae Katherine (Paetkau) Schroeder
Born—October 2, 1994
Died in Christ—April 13, 2022
ALIVE IN CHRIST FOR EVER!

See, He is not here. He has risen, just like He said.
Matthew 28:6

Sunday, June 28th, 2022
I find myself seeking Lanae everywhere.
Wherever I look, she is nowhere to be found. The grave, where her body lays, does not bring me any relief, any comfort. Only the Word of God brings me hope—cheering—celebrating—hope. Up and out of that grave in Cochrane, from the field beside Big Hill—will come our precious daughter with an exclamation of TRIUMPH! Her feet will jump and run on this earth. The same feet will be back, only then they will be the perfect-forever-kind of feet.

Jesus told us He would be back and that those who died in Christ, would be the first to rise to meet Him. In the same way He went, He will come again. The best—THE VERY BEST— the renewed Heaven and the renewed Earth— are yet to come!

July 2nd, 2022

Part of grief, I am discovering, is forgiving. In order to heal, I need to forgive Lanae—but even more, I need to forgive myself. I can't really let go without giving myself and Lanae grace. In order to stop protecting the place where I hurt the most, I need to acknowledge it, fully look it in the face, and then let it be what it is—broken, fractured, not finished, messy, incomplete.

The week before Lanae left for her backcountry ski trip, she came upstairs from her basement suite and sat at our kitchen table. I cautiously wanted to help her change her mind about this next adventure.

"Lanae, why do you want to go on this ski trip?

Why do you need to go right now?

Can it wait?

Can it be done another time?

It's Alicia's gender reveal next Thursday. If you go, you will miss it. Could you make it work to be there?

Please don't go, Lanae. This is so important to Alicia. She really wants you to be there.

No, it can't take place on Friday. Garrett is working.

Please Lanae--could you wait and do this ski trip next year?"

The only words I can remember now are:

"No mom... I've pretty much decided that I'm going. Only if the weather turns bad, the forecast changes, will I not go. I've been praying about it, and I really feel that this is the time to do this trip. I've been hoping to do this Guy Hut ski thing since last year. I really want to do this. This opportunity came up, and I want to go."

I had no more reasoning to use with Lanae.

I moved on.

I regret not trying harder. Why didn't I insist on her reconsidering?

Why didn't I talk to her with Logan there?

Why didn't I bring John into the conversation as well?

I felt no peace—but I let it go. I moved on in my mind. This was my default setting, my habit—to rationalise—"well her mind is made up—there's nothing I can do to get her to change her mind—I need to let her go".

As I look at that last photo of Lanae, taken by the skier behind her a few moments before she stepped into eternity, I want to scream—"NO! NO SWEETIE! DON'T GO!!!"

Please don't go… I love you…

I don't want you to leave right now.

It's too early.

It will mean the end of your marriage to Logan.

We need you!

So many people need you to stay a little while longer—Dad, Alicia, Daniel, your youth group girls, your friends, all the horses you work with, the dogs you walk, the grandmas you love to talk with, mom hugs you love to give, the crazy dad gifts you make, the pen art to draw and fill with splashes of colour—they will all miss you.

We do all miss you here—your love, your laughter, your artwork, your energy—it's all still rebounding off the walls—but I can't find you.

To just hear your voice…

To just see your feet running down the street…

To see your legs pumping your bike pedals away from our house…

I loved you so much— so deep— so wide.

Therefore my grief is so deep—so wide.

Now I look at the picture—and my body lurches with a scream.

PLEASE.

DON'T.

GO!

I pause…

God's love now covers what I was lacking.

God was doing an end run on me that day. He was blocking my voice—blocking my will.

He was doing it out of love and goodness. Love for me. Love for Logan. Love for my family. Love for her world—the world of Lanae.

I need to forgive God for taking my Sweetie.

God, please help me.

I need to forgive myself. I need to borrow from God's bank account of grace—and take all the forgiveness I need, to apply to this pain. I need to let it soak in and cleanse me—and change my mind about myself.

Could I do that? Could I give myself that grace?

Now is the time to heal—to acknowledge that it's not my fault—to NOT paint this tragedy with the same paintbrush as the childhood story of my pain.

IT'S NOT MY FAULT!

I CAN STOP BLAMING MYSELF!

Lanae was a grown woman. She made her own choices. I could suggest she not go—but ultimately the choice was hers.

I KNOW GOD IS GOOD.

This death of my loved one, my beloved Sweetie, will no longer have a hold on me.

I will heal!

I will be made whole!

I will move on with Joy in remembering her! I'm looking forward to what is yet to come. My big hug is coming!

July 8th, 2022

It feels like the calm before the storm, the feeling in the air this morning.

I am missing Lanae intensely—being haunted by her absence.

I have moments of pain when I can feel and see in my mind's eye, the moment she fell.

Lanae isn't one to yell when out of control. I think she instantly knew that there was nothing to do but call on Jesus—and I am sure she did. His presence must have been so real.

Alicia (her younger sister) believes that in an instant Lanae would have known she was going to die.

She would have surrendered her body to it as she fell. Rather than screaming she was perhaps quiet—no—she would have prayed.

There were maybe only seconds before she hit her head on the outcropping of rock on the mountain face, knocking her unconscious, causing her to suffer a brain bleed and massive swelling. Her spirit sensed God's presence—His glory.

She saw herself fall, so gently—like a feather being laid down on the snow.

She fell slower than the cornice, which had been the size of half of a football field. She rested peacefully on top of the category three avalanche she had created. It was a miracle she was not buried under the debris.

Did the BC Parks employee reporting to Global News find this incredible?

For I am persuaded beyond doubt (am sure) that neither death nor life, nor angels nor principalities, nor things impending and threatening nor things to come, nor powers, nor height nor depth, nor anything else in all creation will be able to separate us from the love of God which is in Christ Jesus our Lord.
Romans 8:38-39

My Sweetie loved Jesus.
Jesus loved her.
Nothing could separate her from His love.

Lanae (front) and three of the other four skiers on Tuesday, April 12, 2022

Jesus was there with her. She had a fraction of a second to weigh the pros and cons of staying or going home with her Lord.
She chose to go home.
Her Garmin smart watch was like a physical diary, left behind. It showed her heart rate during her physical activity. The watch captured the sudden rise in adrenaline as she began to fall—seconds of intense heart rate as she dropped at a speed of 80 km/h—then a return back to her exercise rate, then a decline to a resting heart rate of 40 beats per minute. She was unconscious.

The watch showed eight minutes of resting heart rate, and then the heart rate slowly ebbed away.

She didn't suffer.

She was gently laid down—watched over—then carried home with her Jesus. She was safe—free.

Her last journal entry on April 10th said, *"How much longer Lord till you take us home?"*

She longed for Heaven.

Her journal notes from Pastor Joel's sermon were on how to share the gospel of Jesus with others. She wrote a whole page on that topic. One of the skiers later shared that she had spoken in detail with him, all about Jesus, on Tuesday, the night before the accident.

Her journal entry of April 7th, recorded her doubts about the ski trip.

"I make my plans—but You are the One who determines my steps. Thank You that You open and shut doors, that You give me wisdom. So, God, I maybe just did something really foolish and irresponsible. I e-transferred $150 to a guy that I haven't met yet to go on a kind of extreme ski trip next week, in which the weather may or may not be great. Even in good visibility, this is a hard trip. This is an experience that I have been asking You for— please make it crystal clear if I should go or not. That it would be obviously snowing or not. Because if a storm/precipitation is predicted and high winds, then I'm not going. It would be a bad idea to do that route in low visibility, even with GPS. If that is the case, please provide enough work to make up for the $150 that I just spent. Thanks that in the light of eternity, our lives are so much more valuable than $150."

It took two hours for the search and rescue helicopter to arrive at the base of the glacier. Lanae lay peacefully waiting—already asleep— not struggling—not crying out—not trying to get her backpack off.
She was asleep—already pain-free—perfect— complete—her race finished—being held in the sweet embrace of her precious Saviour.
I imagine in Heaven, there would have been many lined up, milling around, coming into the

huddle, waiting to hug her and welcome her home. They would've greeted her with big grins and hearty hellos. My dad first—and my mom—then aunt Sal—all lovingly tucking her into their embraces. Aunt Wilma too—and Granny Schmidt, Helena. Lanae was named after Helena—"Light". Her Grosspa (grandpa) Peter and her Grossma Katherine would be there. She was named after her Grossma as well.

We prayed Lanae would be a reflection of God's light—to magnify His joy—His truth—and show the world that He is the source of light—the only light in the darkness for all humanity.

Lanae lived well and was loved well on earth. There were so many to welcome her on the other side—as the boat left this shore—and grew tiny as it headed east over Jordan—carrying its precious cargo—arriving safely on Heaven's shore—to the cheers of "well done," and clapping and exclaiming, "You made it!" So many congratulations. So much joy!

She is home. My Sweetie is safely Home.

July 15th, 2022
God, please grant me the serenity to accept the things I cannot change, the courage to change the things I can, and the wisdom to know the difference. These are the words from the plaque that hung on the wall in my childhood home.

July 16th, 2022
"Real gold does not fear the fire."

July 17th, 2022
Did you know God has a book in which every life that was ever lived, is written?

Your eyes have seen my unformed substance;
And in Your book were all written
The days that were appointed for me,
When as yet there was not one of them [even taking shape].
How precious also are Your thoughts to me, O God!
How vast is the sum of them!
If I could count them, they would outnumber the sand.
When I awake, I am still with You.
Psalm 139: 16-18

July 22, 2022

Lanae has now been in Heaven one hundred days.

It seems impossible that it's been that long—and at the same time it seems like just a few days. The police came to our door the evening of April 13th. I dread every Wednesday now, when the clock shows 8:15 PM.

The screams are still reverberating in my ears, "NO! NO! NOT MY SWEETIE!"

86

For I know that my Redeemer and Vindicator lives,
And at the last He will take His stand upon the earth.
Even after my [mortal] skin is destroyed [by death],
Yet from my [immortal] flesh I will see God,
Whom I, even I, will see for myself,
And my eyes will see Him and not another!
My heart faints within me.
Job 19:25-27

July 23, 2022
This is the truth that I am standing on today—that Lanae will one day stand on the Earth with Jesus—first in the Millennium—then in the new Heaven and on the new Earth. It will be her self-same hands— and her feet—her beautiful legs will run—they will once again climb—and scale unimaginable heights.
It has been one hundred days—ONE HUNDRED DAYS!—of being shocked, grieved, crying at random moments—of having my stomach churn and my womb ache. My baby is gone.
I've been seeking the Lord—asking Him to help me move forward—asking him to turn my mourning into Joy. Sometimes He does. Sometimes I choose to hold on to the pain, to remain angry.

Have I been believing a lie? I thought my suffering was not as great—not as significant—as one who was martyred for their faith.

A breakthrough came as I walked, thought, prayed, and read *Safely Home* by Randy Alcorn.

God exposed the lie.

My suffering—which is far greater than just this recent pain—goes back to when I was born. I lived with a dysfunctional mother who battled schizophrenia. God showed me, through Elizabeth Elliot's talk, that my pain is not for nothing. All the suffering and pain that comes to the child of God is not in vain. I will one day come forth as gold.

> ***For I consider [from the standpoint of faith] that the sufferings of the present life are not worthy to be compared with the glory that is about to be revealed to us and in us!***
> ***Romans 8:18***

God hears my prayers. They are held in a bowl in Heaven. One day, I will see the answers poured out. He saves my tears in a bottle. My thought is that maybe—one day—those tears will be poured out to bring healing to others. He is close to me—holding me. I can trust Him. If you, dear reader, are in pain—suffering—I want you to know that He sees you.

He is holding you close. He is bearing your pain. He is with you. He will come through for you. He loves you and He will wipe away every tear. He will never forget you—He knows you. He has inscribed your name on the palm of His hand. One day, you will see Him. The spiritual will become physical. It won't be long now.

aporoziah, Ukraine 2006

The Lord is near to the heartbroken
And He saves those who are crushed in spirit
(contrite in heart, truly sorry for their sin).
Psalm 34:18

Jesus, I need to let You hold me now. I need to let Your comfort replace the grief in my heart. I need to let Your Words of peace penetrate my thoughts.

I need to let You into the pain, the loss, the grief, the despair I have been carrying.
I need to kneel before You and let my grief pour out.
I am sitting at an empty chair—imagining You sitting there—I'm holding my Bible—crying—pouring out everything before You. Lord, I want to enter Your rest. Fill me with your peace that goes beyond understanding. I want others to know there is peace—there is hope—there is life beyond this world.

"Leanne, time to come on into my Joy. I am the gate. Open the door and I will come to give you that peace—but more—the JOY!" Thank You for this greater intimacy with You, Lord. I receive all that You are giving to me. I am no longer screaming inside. I choose Your healing, and Your wholeness.

Blessed [refreshed by God's grace] are those who mourn, for they will be comforted.
Matthew 5:4

Chapter Five

My Sweetie

Monday, August 8th, 2022

It's cold… or rather I'm cold. I'm sitting on a bench by the Bow River in Cochrane. It's 8:00 in the evening. Even on some days that are warm, I feel chilled, as if I can't warm up because my insides are frozen like an ice block. It's the 34th anniversary of John proposing to me. After a moon-lit walk, he gave me a beautiful diamond ring as we stood near the Bez Hotel in Saskatoon, Saskatchewan. I should be having warm fuzzy memories, but instead I feel choked with sadness. If I had known back then what would transpire years later, would I have begged God for kids? Would I have gone to our pastor after three years of struggling with infertility to ask him to anoint John and I with oil for healing? Would it have been better to remain barren, rather than to have lost a child?

These thoughts have been brooding darkly in me for days. I have been resisting Joy—again. I would rather remain angry with God.

Lanae Katherine Paetkau was born in the Bow Island Alberta Health Care Centre—11:30 AM on Sunday, October 2, 1994. Thirty-two hours of brutal labour went by and Lanae finally came, as my nurse, Anne Sigglekow, prayed over me for a miracle.

Right as the sermon started at the E. Free Church in Bow Island, Alberta, the phone rang. Someone answered it in the church office and as the guest speaker, Pastor Colin Creighton (a friend of ours) said, he may as well have stopped there. All were waiting to hear the news. After the sermon, someone came and shared about Lanae's birth. A cheer went up, with a lot of clapping. People were so happy Lanae had arrived safely to their associate pastor's home. She was home at last with her mom and dad. We had prayed, waited and hoped for her for three years. Our joy soared at bringing our little blonde bundle home. So many cute pink receiving blankets—so many cute fuchsia-pink outfits from the church baby shower.

One week later—Thanksgiving Sunday—I sang to her as I held her in my arms—"A sunbeam, a sunbeam, Jesus wants you for a sunbeam…you'll be a sunbeam for Him." My precious Lanae. You were a beautiful sunbeam for Jesus.

As a little girl, my dad's colleague named his newborn girl, Linea. I have treasured that name in my heart since I was eight years old. In a book of names, I discovered Lanae means the same as Helena, my Granny Schmidt's name. The meaning of her name is 'light'. I knew in my heart that that's what God wanted her to become. This is Lanae's life verse.

Let your light shine before men, in such a way that they may see your good deeds and moral excellence, and (recognize, honor, and) glorify your Father who is in heaven.
Matthew 5:16

She was dedicated to Jesus on THAT stage in her cute blue dress with the white ruffle.
I marched her down THAT aisle, out the front door, across the street towards home, when she was disobeying me in church as an 18-month-

old toddler. She rode her tricycle from THAT green house, over to the Thurston's, for a glass of milk and a cookie. So many memories of her in our home town.

Lanae was a bundle of energy who had her mind made up on many things. A born leader, strong-willed and determined, she gave me new definitions to the term "high need parenting". She wanted to be held by mommy and mommy alone. We went with attachment parenting against many opinions and judgments, and we let her be held, cuddled, nursed, and dandled on our knees. God spoke to me that my love poured out would certainly not spoil her, but rather it was exactly what she needed.

I was so grateful to be a mom and have God's guidance and wisdom to know how to parent her.

John and I walked in His wisdom, bringing her up to know Jesus. When Lanae was three years old, we lived in Kyiv, Ukraine, studying Russian. I think it was the end of December 1998, when my Sweetie said, "Mommy, here you go. Here's my soother. I don't need it anymore."

"What?" I replied. "But Sweetie, how are you going to manage falling asleep tonight?"

"Oh, I will be okay. Jesus will help me. I just sang Him into my heart."

I was stunned—and just quietly took the soother out of her hand. She ran off to continue playing. I looked for a place to hide her beloved soother, soskah—up high—just in case she cried for it later that night. She didn't. She never asked for it again. I shouldn't have been surprised. Her relationship with Jesus proved to be genuine and she showed us that He was all she needed.

Lanae grew up in Sumy, Ukraine as a missionary kid (an MK), the oldest of three children. When she was introduced to her kindergarten teacher in Kyiv, during our language school years, the teacher asked, "What kind of name is that for a girl? We can't properly use her name in sentences. In our language, a girl's name must end in "a" or "yah". Go home and see what you can come up with for tomorrow."

So, outside of our inner circle, our Lanae was known as Lanea. When she went off to college, she wanted others to know her as Lanea. I wonder if in Heaven, will I have the privilege to have Lanae share with me her new name that she has received from Jesus?

He who has an ear, let him hear and heed
what the Spirit says to the churches.
To him who overcomes (the world through
believing that Jesus is the Son of God), to Him
(the privilege of eating) some of the hidden
manna,
and I will give him a white stone, with a new
name engraved on the stone
which no one knows except the one who
receives it.
Revelation 2:17

Lanae homeschooled most of her school years.
It was so difficult to teach her how to read.
Everything took more effort. Have you ever
tried to push a shopping cart with stuck wheels?
That's what it was like parenting Lanae. Once
she learned how to read, she loved reading. She
was so creative with writing and drawing. My
Sweetie was an artist before she could read. At
two and a half, she drew people, animals, and
trees that you could recognize. In middle
school, she spent hours drawing and sewing
things for herself and others. She was so
creative.

ome of Lanae's doodling from her journal

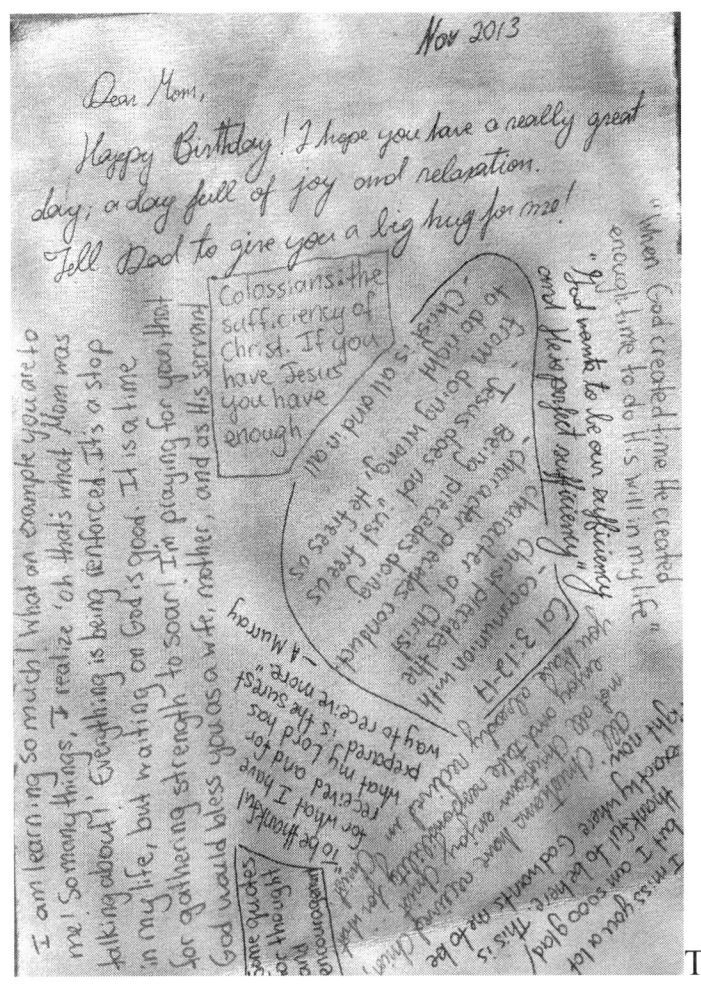

T

here are three things that describe my Lanae:

ummer 1998 Celebrating Lanae's Recovery from a serious illness

She was adventurous.

She relished a new opportunity, a new challenge, and the possibility of growing. Whatever she put her mind to do, she strove to do her best. She was not one to shy away from taking a risk, but she was a calculated risk taker. Backcountry skiing had become a favourite winter sport for her and Logan, both for the challenge and the opportunity. Summers were spent hiking and climbing deep in the mountains. Many times, when they came home, they would show pictures – and inevitably there was snow because they had been up that high. She and Logan were "adventure buddies", each bringing their skills and abilities together in order to create memories and do ministry.

102

She loved Jesus.

Her Lord and Saviour was at the forefront in all of her relationships and conversations. She was one who was confident in her faith, and ready and willing to share when God opened a door. She loved spending time with Junior High students and teens, helping them to grow as individuals and to learn more about God and grow closer to Him. Her heart was soft towards the broken and abused, and she loved serving those who were impacted by this trauma. She volunteered at a local women's ministry in Calgary, helping women learn how to be physically healthy, taking them on hiking trips into the mountains, and sharing the love of Christ with them and helping them to be spiritually healthy. Growing up in Ukraine gave her a heart to serve, as God gave her opportunities to grow, learn and to be involved in so many different ways.

She was restless for Heaven.
Lanea loved being in nature, as it was the closest she could get to Heaven here on Earth. We live in a world filled with pain and evil, and this wore at her heart. She had written many times in her journals, asking God "How long until You take us home?" As a missionary kid, you don't fit exactly into any culture – not the culture of your passport nor the culture that you live and serve in. So home is always a bit of a question, and as she grew in her faith, she realised that until Heaven, she would never really be home. She wanted God to use her time here on earth for Him, but she was ready to go whenever He gave the word.

Lanea wasn't perfect. She struggled in many areas and had many difficult times over her years. It was her faith in God that kept her moving forward through those times, to work at rebuilding that which had been broken and to look forward to what God might do. From a human perspective, she died much too young and there was so much before her. From an eternal perspective, her life was in God's hands and He was faithful to give her the strength and the time to do what she had been called to do. God doesn't measure effectiveness in years, and thus we can rest knowing that His timing is perfect and His will is good. We rest knowing that she is in the hands of her loving Saviour, and that she is home.

Three things that describe my Sweetie is a message from John, Lanae's Dad.

Every year, every birthday, was a celebration of her life. The Graham-Paetkau alliance were overcomers and our little sunshine was storming the gates of hell with her no-nonsense approach to everyday life—with her zeal for Jesus. She let her light shine before men so they would see her good deeds and glorify God the Father. She didn't hide her light under a bushel—No! She shone and shone and shone some more—even when people misunderstood our little MK (Missionary Kid). She shone and never missed a beat at the thought that people didn't get her. She was in the process of growth, and sometimes sent confusing signals from within one culture to the next. The Lord graciously brought people into her life who loved her just the way she was—were even drawn to her through her teens and into young adulthood.

My Sweetie, being the sunbeam she was, brought healing to my wounded spirit. I gladly offered her back. "Here You go, Jesus! Be glorified through her life!" But now… darkness. Someone… something… has snuffed out my shining ray of sunlight. Never once did it occur to me to ask that God would be glorified in her death. Here I am God—I now surrender her to death so others can come to the moment of knowing Jesus as their all in all. I give her to You—in life and now in death. I surrender—I yield—I offer. She is not mine—

her life—her smile—her joy—her "Wow! That's so cool!"

God, I give you her speed—her enthusiasm—her energy—her ability to impact a person in conversation with caring questions about them—to love on them as Jesus loved them. These beautiful attributes of Lanae were never mine to hold on to. They were all offered up to Jesus—and now—as always—are offered up again. To You, Lord Jesus, may they continue to ripple out—touching lives as they go—just as the wind creates a wave in the tops of ripened wheat fields.

From Lanae's journal…
Little choices matter…
The small things…
What we worship…false
religions…worshipping idols…
What we do
Leads other people.
Do I think that my personal, worship,
daily life choices don't have an impact?
I am leaving a legacy whether I like it or
not!

Lanae used a permanent marker to draw her artwork and the words, Talitha Kum—"Little girl I say to you, arise"—on her car, which Lanae eventually sold exactly as it was. Lanae completed two years of Bible School— the first year at Torchbearers Bodenseehoff in Germany, the second year at Miller College of the Bible, Sunnybrae, in British Columbia. She met Logan Schroeder there. They were good friends for two years before they dated and married November 5th, 2016.

It was the week of the 6th of April, 2022. I was imploring Lanae not to go on the ski trip. Monday, April 10th, I felt a dark cloud of oppression hanging over me. I knew there was a battle in the Heavenly realms, and I needed to pray. I thought it could be because of the chaos in Ukraine due to the Russian Invasion. Tuesday I was physically sick. My stomach was groaning in pain all day long. I had to go to work Tuesday evening—and there I asked my friend to pray. I told her something is shifting. Something big is coming. Something is really off.
Wednesday, April 13th was a fun day of busily helping many people. John and I watched Liam—our precious grandson—while our son-in-law and daughter Alicia went for her ultrasound for baby Jones #2. We tried to send a parcel to John's brother in Romania. We didn't have enough weight for the shipment—so we quickly drove to Costco to get more groceries. While I shopped, I thought of Lanae the whole time—she had lived with her Aunt and Uncle and knew them well. The items we chose that day had to be good quality. I kept saying to myself: "What kind of oatmeal does Lanae buy? What kind of peanut butter would

Lanae choose?" At that same time, she was falling off the mountain and dying on a glacier. Our receipt from the checkout showed 11:54 AM, April 13th, 2022. She had already arrived, safely home.

Tuesday, August 12th, 2022
Yesterday was my day of surrender—again. I completely yielded up what happened to the Lord. I gave my Sweetie back to God— submitting all that took place to Him. I gave up fighting against reality.
"Here I am, Lord. Do with me as you wish. I am not my own. I am yours. Take all of me— all that I am—all that I'm not—all that I have— all my dreams, desires, and expectations. I surrender them all to you. I am not my own. I have been bought with a price. Here I am Lord. Send me."
So many years of parenting. So many prayers. So many ecstatic joyful moments—such a mountaintop experience to see her so happy walking down the aisle on John's arm to Logan, her waiting groom.

I was on cloud nine.

110

She was so beautiful.

I had never seen a more beautiful bride until then.

I am angry at God and having a hard time letting go.

Later, in the months of May and June, I had begun to read *Heaven* and *Safely Home* by Randy Alcorn. These books gave me some new insights into what Heaven is like. Now I had many things to mull over and talk with God about. My joy and excitement grew exponentially as I allowed myself to imagine Lanae there in Heaven. I could see the delight on her face— and—I was finally free to start picturing my mom, my dad, my granny whom I'd never met, my aunt Sal, my Aunt Wilma— in Heaven. Oh, the Joy! The pure rapturous delight. Oh, the singing! The adventures. The assignments. The perfect love poured out on the once tragically orphaned children from Ukraine and other war-torn countries. Heaven is more than I had ever dreamed of; more real, more vibrant, more alive with life, than our three dimensional earth, with a fourth dimension of time. We who are part of the family of God, are headed to an eternity in a real PLACE, that is much more than a long, drawn out worship service. I have now become very curious about Heaven, and am so eager to meditate on all the passages in the Bible that talk about our future destination.

We travelled to Bow Island, August 7th, for John to do pulpit supply in one of our supporting churches. Driving back to Cochrane, after the weekend was over, we eventually neared our mountains. I was filled with such loathing. They continuously mock me, and I have no admiration for them right now. I am left with an emptiness—a longing.

All I want to do is go Home. How much longer, Lord?

When will the last Gentiles get on the boat and then the door close?—just like you closed the door on the Ark.

Grade 12 Graduation from Centre for Learning online school in Okotoks, Alberta

Oh, my Sweetie. Jesus made the pathway up for you. You have now graduated to Heaven. While you were yet a sinner, Jesus died for you. My feelings for you help me understand in a small way Jesus' love for me. His willingness to die so mankind could live is amazing. You trusted Him with your life. You were in the best Hands possible—the best position to take on life and death. You were prepared in the best way for that moment of departure. You were safe—abiding in Christ.

I am the Vine; you are the branches.
The one who remains in Me and I in him
bears much fruit,
for [otherwise] apart from Me [that is, cut off
from vital union with Me]
you can do nothing.
John 15:5

I believe that even in death, Lanae's life will lead others to Life. But now, the grief seems too much—too long to bear—too great—too sticky. It feels like a gooey mess—a pot of black tar, pouring continuously on my head, till I can't breathe. Please Lord, release me from this painful pit. I want to be free—to be washed clean from this sticky, dark, blinding mess. I want to be able to see—to lift my head and sing. I mean really sing—belt it out from the bottom of my lungs in freedom and sing with joy! I will sing this way on the day I see my Jesus face to face—my Saviour and best friend.

But it seems so far away, Lord. This road has gone on for so long. Every new turn has had another painful part where I feel slapped down—so broken, I feel like I am unable to rise up again. This has been the lowest punch. I can't catch my breath. Lord, help me to stand—to be healed.

I believe God is telling me: "STAND UP!" What does He mean?

"STAND UP, LEANNE! YOU ARE HEALED! She is with Me—your Sweetie is with Me—whole and healed—happy and glorious—not a blemish—not a sigh. She is here because of you. You pointed her to Me all the way. You got her to home base. My jewel would not have made it here without you leading her to Me. You did it, Leanne! Well done, my good and faithful servant—faithfully administering all the good things I had entrusted to you—your kids—your beloved ones.

> You did well!!
> Be healed! Be comforted!
> Be held! Be hugged!
> Be still in my arms!
> Be at rest! Be at peace!

She is safe, sound, and happy—rejoicing—adventuring with her beautiful feet that will one day be filled again with the selfsame atoms, molecules, and cross-filled DNA. She will be and is your Lanae. She is My jewel—My precious one. She is so beautiful—and you did so well with what I entrusted to you. Now I am multiplying her one hundred fold—ONE HUNDRED FOLD!!!"

Lanae was so grateful for what the Lord did in her and through Arise, the extreme hike that she went on with some church ladies. She wrote

that God showed her things that were hindering her. She was able to let go of so much. Thank You, Lord Jesus, for surrounding Lanae with people who poured into her, and helped her to seek after You and rest in You even more.
I am saddened by the condition—the state—the attitude—of my heart today. It is only one of the forms or costumes that grief shows up in. Anger and despair like to make unwelcome appearances.
I have a choice. I can trust God and His Word, or I can stay here and drown in despair—more entrenched in my depression. Or I could step into the knowing that my sweet Lanae is really and truly ALIVE!—even more than me—in the presence of Jesus. She is there!

> *The Lord GOD is my strength (my source of courage, my invincible army);*
> *He has made my feet (steady and sure) like hinds' feet*
> *And makes me walk (forward with spiritual confidence) on my high places (of challenge and responsibility).*
> *Habakkuk 3:19*

It is time. Time for me to let go of this broken earthly Lanae, and embrace the restored heavenly Lanae, knowing our relationship goes on. It's not over. There will be a future time of laughing, hugging, running, and dancing with

Lanae as her mom, and she as my precious forever daughter. I will go to her one day because Jesus' blood has opened the way for me. I am stepping in.

The LORD gave, and the LORD has taken away; Blessed be the name of the LORD. Job 1:21b

laneasunshine

Chapter Six

Family

umy Grace Camp, Sumy, Ukraine July 2003

Message John wrote to our newsletter and prayer partners (Lanae's Dad – written April 15th, 2022)

As I sit to write this, I just can't believe the words I have to say. Our daughter Lanea (Lanae), our first-born child, celebrated Easter Sunday in person with our Risen Saviour. Lanea died Wednesday, April 13th in a backcountry skiing accident. She was with a group of experienced backcountry skiers, deep in the Rocky Mountains in BC, when the snow

–the cornice—gave way near the peak of a summit that they were on. Lanea fell around 400 metres—about the height of two Calgary towers. She and her husband Logan are experienced climbers and backcountry skiers. Logan wasn't able to get the time off work on short notice and thus he was not there when this happened.

As we hear more of what happened two things have become clear.

First, it was an accident. Lanea at the moment was in the lead breaking trail for the group. It is very evident that whomever was first in line would have fallen, as there was no indication of the danger. As our daughter Alicia said when we broke the news to her, "No, not Lanae, it can't be Lanae, she is too careful". Logan and Lanae did risky things, but always calculated and thought through. So, whomever was first would have died.

Second, Lanae was the only believer in the group, and knowing our daughter she would have already been sharing her faith with the other members.

God reminded me of two things the morning after Lanae went home. First, God doesn't measure effectiveness in length of time. Jesus ministered for three years. Lanae lived her life 27.5 years to the fullest for God, and her life made an impact for the Gospel. Secondly, every parent's desire is that their children finish well. Lanae finished well. She ran the race before her with her gifts, abilities, flaws, and scars, and she has finished well.

anae found dad's cool object lesson sunglasses and dad found his old college glasses.

Please pray especially for our son in law Logan. They were married for 5 1/2 years, and he is grieving deeply and rejoicing greatly. He was gone doing ministry when the police came to our door Wednesday evening to break the news. So, we were the ones to share with him Lanae's stepping into eternity. A few hours after we told him the news he told us,

"I have seen God save Lanea numerous times, she was able to pull out of dangerous situations. If God had wanted to save her this time, He would have. God is good, and I need to trust Him with His plan."

We hold to the hope of the resurrection—we do not grieve without hope—for we have a living Saviour in whose presence our daughter is at this moment. I am grieving deeply the loss of Lanae, yet rejoicing greatly; she finished her race on earth well. I have my good days and my bad moments, which is progress. My grief is as one who has hope that is a solid expectation: I will be seeing her again soon! I know that at this moment she is enjoying the presence of Jesus and is waiting for us to catch up. As a child, she always wanted to run ahead. Well, she just ran ahead and got home before I did. One way that I look at it as well, is that Lanae was on the early train and she is waiting at the train station for her family. Our train is on its way, and soon we too will have the joy of seeing Jesus, Lanae and all those who have gone on before us. God has reminded me that He doesn't measure effectiveness in length of years. I am so proud of her and what she accomplished and how she lived for Jesus in her short 27 years on this earth.

ncle Don teaches Lanae how to ride a bike.

We as family—Logan (her husband), Leanne and I, Alicia and Garrett, Daniel all grieve deeply and rejoice greatly.

Grieving deeply…Rejoicing greatly
(John – July 11th update)

A few months have already passed without our daughter here with us on this earth. April 13, 2022 will always be a day that will be etched in our memories – the day Lanae went home to be with Jesus.

So what do we say now? We say that we continue to grieve deeply and continue to rejoice greatly. We have good days with bad moments, rather than good days and bad days—so that can be called progress we guess.

We have many questions – the book of Job in the Bible resonates with us a lot right now, but I kinda think that all the questions I have won't need answering once I get there.

Presently we feel a lot like our two and a half year-old grandson Liam, when he walks down the street with us holding our hand. Liam doesn't know what is coming a block or two away – he is just focused on what is nearby and interesting. He is trusting us to take care of him. So we are like Liam, holding onto the hand of our loving Heavenly Father and trusting Him with today and the future.

Kyiv, Ukraine 1998
We do not grieve as do those who have no hope.
1 Thessalonians 4:13

We grieve deeply…

We have never felt such searing loss or pain—it is literally like we aren't going to be able to take our next breath.

We have been numb—nothing seemed real.

We have been angry—feeling helpless and wanting to break something—to focus our pain on something physical, to do something.

We have felt fear—how will it affect her siblings—how will it affect her husband?

A man's mind plans his way [as he journeys through life],
But the Lord directs his steps and establishes them.
Proverbs 16:9

The last photo of Lanae…a few steps before she fell into eternity

In everything give thanks...
1 Thessalonians 5:16-18

We rejoice greatly...
When I thought of this verse, I didn't want to obey.

But then I began to think we have so much to be thankful for.

We know from the tech gear she was wearing she didn't suffer in her last moments—her home going was peaceful and quick.

Lanae isn't laying in a hospital in a coma, or paralyzed and unable to.....

We were able to have a service.

Only a few short months prior only twenty people could attend a funeral. More than five hundred people physically attended Lanae's celebration of life.

Over five hundred attended on Livestream.

Lanae is in the presence of Jesus.

We KNOW that what is coming is far better than anything we have experienced yet.

Lanae is there, beginning to see, taste, touch and feel all that we someday will.

She has gone before, and we will see her again.

Lanae was five steps from eternity.
We are all five steps from eternity.
My question I ask myself every day is,
"What am I doing with my five steps?"
With love,
John

Alicia, Daniel, and Lanae at home in Sumy,
Ukraine 2012

Alicia (Lanae's Sister)

It almost felt like déjà vu—like I was
expecting to have my parents tell me one day
that Lanae was gone. I just didn't know when it
would happen, but I knew. The older Lanae got,
the more risks she would take, going on more

and more extreme adventures. I have a fear of, "but what if?" Lanae didn't live that way. I knew she would put herself in risky, dangerous situations—she went three to four times a week to the mountains. My parents coming to my door that day with the news that Lanae had been killed in an outback skiing accident, was a surprise to me, and yet it wasn't. When I opened the door that early morning, I already knew it was because of Lanae.

Lanae and Alicia - Kyiv, Ukraine Fall 1998

It was on my heart to do something to express my love for my sister. I decided I wanted to look after the flowers for the funeral service. I went to Panda flowers in Cochrane with Lanae's sister-in-law, Lauren. We picked out bright oranges, pinks, and sunflowers. I wanted Lanae to be surrounded by a vibrant garden.

They looked so beautiful. So many donated money from all over the world for the flowers—for the funeral. From our war-torn Ukraine where we had grown up and lived for seventeen years, gifts of money surprised me and I cried with gratefulness for their sacrifice. Thousands came in. It was a gift from God. When the funeral was over, I went home tired and empty. The stillness was too quiet after all the voices of five hundred plus people that came to Lanae's service to say goodbye. I was sitting on the edge of my bed, resting, worn out, and a clear inaudible voice in my head said, "Thanks Alicia for the flowers!" I wanted to doubt the voice, but it came not of my own volition, and I wondered silently to myself if it was even possible. The Heaven that Lanae now calls Home, is blessed with God's amazing grace, to give us here on earth, glimpses of reality there and His LOVE for us who are left a little while longer on this earth.

Daniel (Lanae's Brother)

The day that I received the phone call from my parents that Lanae had died, I was studying in England. I was called into the Director's office at noon to wait for a call from my dad.

When mom told me that Lanae had gone home to be with Jesus, the shock hit me, not physically, but emotionally. My sister was gone, and there was a huge emptiness inside. I sat there, and started to cry, and it dawned on me that this was really happening; the thing that you think will never happen, happened. It happened to our family. We were no longer a family of five…Lanae was no longer on the earth.

The song, *Untitled Hymn,* by Chris Rice, began to go through my head…

"When you fall, fall on Jesus".

I said, "Mom and Dad…Lanae fell on Jesus."

I wept a lot.

I realised that Lanae had met our Saviour Jesus…she was really there.

As I turned to leave the director's office, I saw a painting on the wall—the Father hugging the prodigal son coming home.

That was happening right in Heaven right then—the Father was hugging Lanae. She was home. The Father was there for me too—comforting me.

I went to my favourite tree, sat there, and wept.

What next?

I needed to decide what to do.

Would I go home to Canada? I knew I needed to be there for my sister's funeral.

The numbness settled in and I felt weak. Friends at my supper table asked what was wrong. They sat with me in my grief—shared my burden with me. The principal stood up and announced that my sister had been killed in a skiing accident, and at some point, I would be going home. I cried as I heard the news from our leader—it seemed more final—more real. I sobbed—and sobbed—and started shaking. People gathered around—put their hands on me and prayed.

God was there for me.

At the end of the school year, many told me Lanae's death profoundly affected their lives. It brought the school community together.

This was the beginning of fruit from Lanae's death.

Sunrise Easter service was four days later at the Joshua Tree just outside Capernwray Hall. We sang as the sun rose. I realised because Jesus had risen from the dead, Lanae too would rise from the dead. In her time, outside of time, SHE ALREADY HAD! SHE WAS ALIVE!!

Lanae's death enhanced my experience at Capernwray. It pushed me closer—towards Jesus. This is so real now! Because of Lanae's death, the Gospel became even more tangible to me.

For me it was the necessity of suffering. God has taught me so much through this time of tragedy and pain. My dad had said, "Either we believe now what God's word says as never before, or we don't believe it at all and it's all for nothing. If we believe that His word is true and that Heaven is real, and Lanae is in a real place there in the presence of God, then we need to live it, and act on it. We need to show that we believe what we believe IS TRUE!"

God has been teaching me so much about suffering.

We don't want to suffer.

We don't like to suffer.

We didn't want Lanae to die. We as people don't want to go through hardship or addiction or war or famine or disease—but it happens! God has been teaching me through this, that there is a purpose for suffering. He works through it and uses it to do His will—to further His Kingdom. He uses suffering to grow us—to refine us—to make us beautiful—to make everything He gives us in His Word—tangible—through hardship.

I've been reading through the book of Job—a man who doesn't know Christ. He lived before the time of Jesus. Job was a man looking for answers. He asked why questions. I'm asking why questions. Why is this happening? Why is the world falling apart? Why are people hating and killing each other? Why am I hurting? Why am I going through this? Why, God? The big question in Job is just why. Why is life like this?

As Job and his "friends" debated, I've noticed that his friends are a lot like the modern church.

They're saying a lot of fluffiness or just not grounded in reality. Job is looking for answers to the big questions in life. The friends are kind of like so many shallow people of our time. There are so many points where Job nails it…he's onto something—but, he doesn't realise Satan is the one punishing him—not God. He says, "Oh no that my disaster has come from the hand of the Lord!" The main thing he's missing is Jesus! I'm reading through Job and agreeing with him. Why are we suffering?

Why?

Job talks about how God seems like an over-demanding persecutor who just analyses our lives all the time, bringing up our sin. Job's like, "You know God when I'm going to die; You numbered my days. You know I'm going to go to the grave and then nothing happens after that. We don't rise again so what's the point? Just leave me alone and let me live the rest of my few days in peace." Then he says this in chapter 14 verse 14, he says "Can the dead live again? If so, this would give me hope through all my years of struggle and I would eagerly await the release of death. You would call and I would answer and You would yearn for me and the work of Your hands. For then You would guard my steps instead of watching for my sins. My sins would be sealed in a pouch and You would cover my guilt." I said to myself: That's Jesus! Jesus does that for us!! That's what Job was missing! He was unaware at that point that the dead would live again. Yes, because of what Jesus did on the cross, I will see Lanae again in heaven. I will rejoice with her and dance with her. I had this picture in my head that when I get to heaven, I'll see Lanae running through a field and I'm going to run to her, pick her up and spin her around fifty times and just hug her and cry for joy. Then I will see Jesus and He will say to me, "Good job! Well done! You made it! You're here!!" Knowing that the dead in Christ live again gives me hope through all my years of struggle. Jesus gives us hope. Our struggles have a purpose—to make His word tangible—so much more real.

My reaction to Lanae's death—how I responded to God—seeing what God was doing in my life—was bearing fruit. Many people around the world sent us messages like, "Lanae's death and her funeral message had such an impact on me. I'm coming back to church. I'm coming back to God. I'm seeking God again." What it did for me at school and for the rest of the community at school and how it enhanced everyone else's experience there is showing me that God is doing so much through Lanae's death. I don't like what has happened, but how can I be mad at God? God is making this into such an amazing, beautiful thing. Lanae got the better end of the deal, because now she's in eternity. She's doing better than all of us. God is doing so much more through us as well--it's like—if Lanae's death means that she's now infinitely better off and her experiences are immensely enhanced, Lanae's death was definitely part of God's good plan.

I miss Lanae. I miss her a lot. I wish I had spent more time with her and made more memories. As a result of Lanae's death, I am looking forward to Heaven SO much more. God gave me a picture when I was still at Bible School in Germany. Heaven will be so beautiful. I will see everyone I've missed. I will see Lanae again. If my mom and dad go before me, I'll see them again. There'll be such rejoicing, hugging, crying and kissing. It's going to be amazing!

When we get to Heaven there will be a feast—the Wedding Supper of the Lamb. We will sit down with Jesus. I can picture this huge table—everyone sitting—all of God's people from all times and places. The spread is amazing—the kind of food that you can't even imagine. We are all sitting there, and the feeling in the room is like we've just been through a war—a great battle. I imagine it to be similar to that which J.R.Tolkien writes about at the end of the Lord of the Rings. The feeling is—oh my goodness—we made it! We did it! Are we all dusty and sweaty and sitting down exhausted? Maybe not, because we will be in our perfect new bodies.

I compare it to the feeling when a huge weight is lifted off of my shoulders--as though I've just come through the battle of battles-- the war of wars that is life here on earth--with all the scars I've accumulated and all the valleys I went through--and seeing how I've grown through it all. I know Christ MORE. The battles of Earth have brought me into a deep, intimate, loving relationship with Him.

I imagine us sitting at the banquet table. Our faith has become sight. We turn to face Jesus, Who is sitting at the head of the table. He's the Honoured One—we are the Guests. He's the Host—we are the Invited. He is the Groom—we are the Bride. He is the Lover—we are the Beloved.

We can tell He's about to say something important so we all quietly—eagerly—wait to hear what He will say. We all lean in. There are SO many people—but it's so quiet you could hear a pin drop. We hold our breath. Jesus looks at all of us. There's a twinkle in His eyes—then a huge grin on His face. He throws His head back and laughs—and laughs—and laughs—a joyous laughter, like we've never heard before. We laugh with Him— rejoicing that the weight has come off of our shoulders– it's the wedding feast laughter—and

we are finally home! I can't wait to experience
that.

Our family - Cochrane, Alberta 2021

*He will swallow up death [and abolish
it] for all time.
And the Lord God will wipe away tears
from all faces,
And He will take away the disgrace of
His people from all the earth;
For the Lord has spoken.
Isaiah 25:8*

Chapter Seven
Logan

November 5, 2016

Lanae spent a year at Bodenseehof Bible School in Germany in 2013-2014, and then returned to Canada, served at Brightwood Ranch Camp for the summer and attended a year at Millar College of the Bible in Tappen Bay, BC (2014-2015).

During that year at school she met her husband, Logan Schroeder. While he continued at school, she lived and worked in the area, serving as a volunteer firefighter in the Blind Bay detachment, serving as a volunteer at her local church, and taking on new challenges and activities.

Lanea and Logan were married on November 5, 2016, beginning a journey together of wonder, challenge, growth and adventure. God gave them the opportunity to spend 6 months overseas in 2018, doing ministry in 6 different countries, with the desire growing to someday be overseas long term. These past few years, Lanea and Logan have been living in Cochrane, AB, working, serving in the local church, camp ministries and in various capacities with volunteer organisations. They love the outdoors, and sought any opportunity they could to spend time in God's backyard (the Rocky Mountains) hiking, climbing, and skiing with friends and acquaintances. Lanea loved the outdoors, and found it a natural place to share the love of Christ and to build into other's lives. She has been training and growing her skills in multiple areas so that she could use them for the sake of the Gospel. She loved to draw and paint that which she saw and to share that with others.

P

hoto taken near Sicamous, British Columbia.
Finally got her to go snowmobiling.

Logan's Message…

The last thing Lanea said to me before she left for her backcountry ski trip in the early morning hours of April 12th was, "Don't forget to eat the leftovers in the fridge!" The next morning when I woke up, I discovered a sticky note that she had put on the mirror in our bathroom. She had written down a quote from a book she was reading that said something to the effect, "Faith says I will remain true to God and His character no matter what He may do". God has challenged me through this to keep trusting in the Lord, and not waver in my faith that God is a Good God. I have watched God save Lanea from harm, and possible death, no less than fifteen times. He pulled her through every time and He could have done it again, if He had wanted to. He knows what is best, and has something BETTER for me and for all of us who love Lanea and miss her.

Photo taken at Enderby Cliffs, British Columbia

142

God is consistent with how He's treated me, and He's consistent with how He has treated His people throughout history; I can't call Him wrong—I can't claim that Lanea was mine. She never really was mine. She was always His girl. I have thanked God multiple times for allowing me to hold His precious daughter for five amazing years.

Message from Lanae's journal …

"God's voice in my head.
Love is the most powerful frequency. He is love.
I put my faith in His love.
Faith opens the door for His frequency.
It is physical, like the electromagnetic field of our bodies.
Unity—the Spirit in me and in Logan.
Logan and I became one.
We are electromagnetically unified.
Love is the frequency. Sin and darkness are the opposites.
Perfect love casts out fear. They are opposite frequencies.
One day I will see Him with my eyes…"

The day we got engaged, near Regina,
Saskatchewan

God has blessed me so much. When I look back
on those five years I have so many good
memories. I just remember them with a smile.
The hard part is moving forward now and
making new memories that she's not part of. It
doesn't make the old memories any less
precious. When I look at the day Lanea died,
God was absolutely as good to me as He
possibly could be. I've struggled with it— I
struggled with it for a while because I wanted
her back! I know I serve a God who raises the
dead. It was Easter time. I was saying to God,
"I know you can do it; can I have her back?"
Then I had to ask myself, what about the impact
her death is having? What about the lives that
are being changed? The only way any of this

could have been easier on me would have been if she hadn't died at all, but then we wouldn't have had any of this impact on myself and hundreds of people around me.

ock Climbing in Crowsnest Pass

The truth is, I'm just a few steps behind Lanea. We are all going to go. Whether it's Christ's return or our own death, from a practical standpoint, they bring about the same result. We get to live in the presence of Jesus, in the place that He has prepared for each one of us, His kids. The question is: how am I going to live? My life is too short to wallow in self-pity. How you live matters. The choices you make every day matter. Press into God. Seek after Him. Any day could be the last one. Live the moment, not the past. Just look at a flower—it blooms. It doesn't worry about trying to be beautiful, it just is for the moment.

I have spent the last four months completely rethinking grief and loss. People are telling me to let go. I'll never let go. Our times together will always affect who I am, what I think and what I've become. When I have so much to celebrate, how can I grieve as the world grieves?

P
hoto taken in Amman, Jordan.

It's important to live as if I have only a few weeks left. I am just a vapour. I am here now, and then I could be gone. I used to really struggle with the question: "God? What is Your will for my life?" Lanea pointed me to 1 Thessalonians in the Bible, saying, "Logan! I know what God's will is for you!! Rejoice always and delight in your faith; be unceasing and persistent in prayer; and in every situation, be thankful and continually give thanks to God."

Message from Lanae's Journal

"I don't know what will happen tomorrow....
but God is good and He provides.
So I will not be afraid."

The Lord is my strength and my song.
He has become my salvation.
Exodus 15:2

Photo taken somewhere in Kananaskis, Alberta.

Message from Leanne—Lanae's Mom:

Logan was a gift from God to Lanae and our family. He was there for our daughter when she went through dark valleys. John and I will always be grateful for his tender care of our precious Lanae.

148

Message from John—Lanae's Dad

I distinctly remember when Logan asked if he could marry Lanae while he and I travelled on a train in Eastern Ukraine. We had spent three weeks together doing ministry at Sumy Grace Camp. It was close to the time for us to part. Logan was staying to do more ministry and I was heading back to Canada. As I looked at Logan, I thought of myself when I asked my father-in-law if I could marry his daughter. I saw myself in Logan—in love, enthusiastic, excited about the future, and having many areas that I needed to grow in. I thought to myself, "Was I ready to get married?" What I saw in Logan was a young man who loved Jesus and he loved my daughter. And I was thankful. Of course, I said yes.

The photo is from Freedom 8848's Fundraiser
on the Summit in Kananaskis

Over the years, I watched as Logan loved my daughter—doing his best to be a man who loved his wife as Christ loved the church. I've watched as they went through good times and hard times. I watched them grow together. I was so amazed that God granted me such a good son-in-law. The character of the man was shown in his daily walk through some very challenging and difficult times. I never expected the valleys they would go through. To watch him stand and show her unconditional love—no matter the circumstances—his

150

kindness and patience—his joy—his support—
it made me so thankful for God's gift to my
daughter and my family.

Chapter Eight

God is Faithful

S

END International Family Conference in Germany 2011

For we know that if the earthly tent [our physical body]which is our house is torn down [through death], we have a building from God, a house not made with hands, eternal in the heavens.
For indeed in this house we groan, longing to be clothed with our [immortal, eternal] celestial dwelling, so that by putting it on we will not be found naked.
For while we are in this tent, we groan, being burdened [often weighed down, oppressed],

not that we want to be unclothed [separated by death from the body], but to be clothed, so that what is mortal [the body] will be swallowed up by life [after the resurrection].
Now He who has made us and prepared us for this very purpose is God, who gave us the [Holy] Spirit as a pledge [a guarantee, a down payment on the fulfillment of His promise].
2 Corinthians 5:1-5

Friday, July 29th, 2022
Yesterday, grief hit again. One moment I was fine—laughing—and the next moment I missed Lanae so much I thought my heart would burst. Grief comes in waves. Tears rolled down my face. I quieted within and asked myself, "What is really going on? How am I doing?"
In the quiet of my mind the thought came—you don't believe—you don't trust—you have unbelief.

What? Where did that come from?
"Is it true Lord? I have disbelief?"
"Yes, My daughter. You are not walking by faith. My word to you is that your daughter is here with me. You cry out saying, "Where is her voice? Her voice seems to be nowhere—there is nothing—it is gone—simply silent." But I have given you My word and my truth—My written WORD—that Lanae, although absent from the body, having folded up her tent,

she left it behind, and is present –VERY PRESENT—with Me. Do you believe me?"

"Yes, Lord. Help me with my unbelief."

It is the perfect timing. I am beginning Hebrews chapter 11. It is the record of those who have gone before us—who faithfully ran their race of life—and are safely home.

What is faith anyways?

Now faith is the assurance (title deed, confirmation) of things hoped for (divinely guaranteed), and the evidence of things not seen [the conviction of their reality—faith comprehends as fact what cannot be experienced by the physical senses]. For by this [kind of] faith the men of old gained [divine] approval.
Hebrews 11:1-2

I have read and accepted God's written Word and spoken Word to me as truth—that Jesus Christ rose from the dead—that He is alive right now in a very real, physical place. He has also revealed to me through His spoken word—to my spiritual ears—to my heart—that where Jesus is, Lanae is. If He is really alive— she is really alive. If He died and rose again— my daughter who died will also rise again. He is the Resurrection and the Life.

t a supporter's home - Home Service 2001

Jesus is seated on His throne on the right hand of the Father.

Lanae is there!! She is hearing His voice—seeing Him—standing in His presence. How amazing.

It was scary to realise I struggled with unbelief. It was good to finally put my finger on it—to actually define it. Then I could hold it up before God and say, "Here it is, Lord. It's unbelief. I'm having a hard time—a struggle really—to believe Lanae is really, actually with You now."

Was I really doubting God?

He answered me—so patiently.

Zaporoziah, Ukraine 2006

Jesus said to her,
"I am the Resurrection and the Life.
Whoever believes in (adheres to, trusts in,
relies on) Me [as Saviour] will live even if he
dies;
and everyone who lives and believes in Me [as
Saviour] will never die.
Do you believe this?"
John 11:25-26

"Well Leanne, you can see now what you are dealing with—it is a struggle. You do not strive with flesh and blood. The battle is against principalities, against powers, against the rulers of the darkness of this world, against spiritual wickedness in high places."

"Oh, Lord…It is a spiritual battle, not a physical one."

"Yes, Leanne…spiritual. Lift up your shield of faith with which you can then put out all the fiery arrows."

"Yes, Lord, this makes sense and frees my conscience. I don't have to receive blame but rather put blame where it belongs—at the feet of Satan who doesn't want me to believe—who doesn't want me to grieve as one with hope—who doesn't want me to draw near to You and depend on Your Word to me.

IN YOU I PUT MY HOPE AND IN YOU I PUT MY TRUST!!! I BELIEVE."

You have turned my mourning into dancing for me;
You have taken off my sackcloth and clothed me with joy,
That my soul may sing praise to You and not be silent.
O Lord my God, I will give thanks to You forever.

Psalm 30:11-12

In My Father's house are many dwelling places. If it were not so, I would have told you, because I am going there to prepare a place for you.
John 14:2

Saturday, July 30th, 2022
I live on one side of death.
There is another side.
I am thanking You for deliverance from death.

Monday, August 1st, 2022
Lanae is an integral part of my daily thoughts. I might look up for a moment and see a cloud that resembles something she would draw. Maybe she did that for me, left a picture for me on the canvas of the sky. It's as if she is saying,
        "Hey, Mom. Hey mom. I'm here! I'm waiting for Resurrection Day! We will all be together soon—celebrating in the presence of Jesus. It's all worth the wait, Mom. It's all worth the suffering, the perseverance, the pain, the sorrow. That has all faded away. Only Joy remains."
It will come to pass—one day.
There were so many days, so many moments in the day when I felt like I couldn't breathe—that I couldn't go on. God, I need Your strength. Lanae was and always will be my Sweetie. She was born as God's answer to the longing of my heart—my grief poured out—my sobbing before the Lord. Now there is a new kind of grief —but there is an awakening coming, that beyond this known physical world, there really is a place prepared for those who love Jesus. My heart is opening up to the possibilities.

I am giving myself the freedom to dream.
I am imagining what it is like for Lanae now—
for the two of us together—to laugh, to explore,
to create, to go on adventures together.
It is all within the realm of endless, perfect,
exciting possibilities of the One who loves us
and created us. He is there to laugh with us and
to cheer us on. Jesus will be the Source of our
constant and continuous joy.

Beyond that—there will be new beginnings—
the new Heaven and the new Earth. We will be
in our beautiful, glorified, resurrected, perfect
bodies.

Meanwhile—I am learning to let go of what
was—so that I can receive what is—and what
will be.

A sob catches in my throat just now as I
glimpse in my memory her smile, her laugh, her
strong, tanned legs running in a race. I was so
proud of her—watching her—so thankful and
delighted and humbled and blessed to be her
mom.

After completing a 24 km trail run near
Canmore, Alberta – Sept 2019

Now, I move on from that same moment—with tears running down my face—wiping my nose—looking up—and seeing what is still unseen—invisible to my mortal eyes.

She is there! It's a real place!
I will catch up to her!
She went on the earlier train—my train hasn't left the platform yet. She'll be waiting on the platform to greet me—to welcome me with her big hug.
Will it be today? God has numbered my days—as He has for each of us.

There is a countdown. My day of going home, of crossing over, is appointed. Your day is appointed—recorded in a book in Heaven before you were conceived.

*And just as it is appointed and destined for all
men to die once
and after this [comes certain] judgment.
Hebrews 9:27*

My day will come—when Jesus calls those who love Him—when He shouts with a loud command—or when I slip through the veil between here and there. If I die, my body will be left sleeping in the dust—waiting for the resurrection.

The time of pain—of letting a beloved child go—came for me. Maybe it will come for you as well one day.

I read Hebrews 12:1-17 as I grieved this week. He laid it on my heart to share this with you. It is the way forward in joy.

Jesus' Words of instruction are powerful.

Father, please keep my spiritual eyes focused on Jesus. I won't give in to despair. The pain is real. The corrective hand of the Lord is upon me. His discipline is His way to disciple me—making me bear more fruit—fruit that will last.

He disciplines me also through the death of Lanae. Because He loves me, I'm accepting of that—simply, finally, submitting myself to it. Let it be done to me as You have planned and allowed.

He disciplines us for our good so that we may share in His holiness. With time, our trials will yield the peaceable fruit of righteousness. Our attitudes—our desires—we'll seek conformity to God's Will and purpose.

Lord, please strengthen my hands and weak knees. Make straight paths for my feet. Set up new systems that will become habitual to bring me daily into Your presence—Your Word. Get me off the couch of mourning-pain where it is so easy to slip into despair.
I believe You want me to be in nature every morning. I have been forever changed by my night of wrestling with You.

I do not want to fall short of God's grace—to miss out on the beauty of what He has for me. I don't want to miss the mark. Even in my pain, my loss, my brokenness, my God has a banquet for me. I do not want to be stuck—eating from the garbage heap of self-condemnation—resulting in despair, depression, and cycling through darkness—again and again.
God has set out a banquet of joy, healing, laughter, dancing, eternity with Him, the new Heaven and a new Earth where righteousness dwells. I'm going there. I'm choosing to open the gate and enter into that joy now rather than wait. I have a birthright. An inheritance. It is mine because of Jesus. I am not going to sell it, give it away, or let someone or something steal it from me. I belong to the family of God. He

chose me and I choose Him back. He is mine and His banner over me is love.

My Lord has brought me through the valley of tears and sorrow. They were in my food night and day. I was saddened over the tragedy of the loss of my firstborn—her pain, her instantaneous pause of her earthly home, the end of all earthly dreams, marriage and friendships.

Now I realise that her loss immediately resulted in gain. I can hear her…

"Come up here Mom… come and see. In your mind's eye—see the beauty—the aroma of life and Jesus and the Father's world. Enter Mom!—even now—before your departure—enter. Isn't it amazing? Isn't it awesome? Isn't it incredible what He has prepared for those who love Him? Enter now, Mom, into your rest and into your Joy! You don't need to wait. You can have it now. It is your birthright. I'm experiencing it now in all of its fullness. Thanks Mom, for introducing me to Jesus—and discipling me always to Him and for Him. He has brought me safely home."

"There is a peace— come weary and tired and worn—there is a peace, to settle your soul, that's been calling you home. You've been so far from Jesus and so close to hell. YOU ARE NOT OF THIS WORLD! STAND UP AND FIGHT!" (Lyrics from Preacher's

Harvest: There Is A Peace, 2018) We don't grieve as those who have no hope.

A handmade card from Lanae

Lanae loved the hymn, *This is my Father's World*.

This is my Father's world,
And to my listening ears
All nature sings, and round me rings
The music of the spheres.
This is my Father's world:
I rest me in the thought
Of rocks and trees, of skies and seas—
His hand the wonders wrought.
This is my Father's world:
The birds their carols raise,
The morning light, the lily white,
Declare their Maker's praise.
This is my Father's world:
He shines in all that's fair;
In the rustling grass I hear Him pass,
He speaks to me everywhere.
This is my Father's world:
Oh, let me ne'er forget
That though the wrong seems oft so strong,
God is the ruler yet.
This is my Father's world,
The battle is not done:
Jesus who died shall be satisfied,
And earth and Heav'n be one.

This hymn expresses the truth that it is God's plan to bring Heaven down to Earth. "Just as God and mankind are reconciled in Christ, so too the dwellings of God and mankind—Heaven and Earth—will be reconciled in Christ. As God and man will be forever united in Jesus, so Heaven and Earth will forever be united in the new physical universe as resurrected beings." (Heaven: Randy Alcorn pg 103)

> "When God walked with Adam and Eve in the Garden, Earth was Heaven's back yard. The new Earth will be even more than that—it will be Heaven itself. And those who know Jesus will have the privilege of living there." (Heaven: Randy Alcorn pg 103)

This photo of sunset in Sumy, Ukraine was sent from Lanae's friend Katya on August 22, 2022.

This is a photo from Freedom 8848 August 20th, 2022. These hikers are wearing t-shirts that were tie-dyed in honour of Lanae. Freedom 8848 is a three-day hike, to raise funds to help those who have been sexually exploited. They have a vision to end sex-trafficking in our world.

August 2022 – Freedom 8848 Participants wearing t- shirts designed in honour of Lanae.

Therefore, since we are surrounded by so great a cloud of witnesses [who by faith have testified to the truth of God's absolute faithfulness], stripping off every unnecessary weight and the sin which so easily and cleverly entangles us, let us run with endurance and active persistence the race that is set before us, [looking away from all that will distract us and] focusing our eyes on Jesus, who is the Author and Perfecter of faith [the first incentive for our belief and the One who brings our faith to maturity], who for the joy [of accomplishing the goal] set before Him endured the cross, disregarding the shame, and sat down at the right hand of the throne of God [revealing His deity, His authority, and the completion of His work].
Hebrews 12:1-2

Chapter Nine

A Labour of Love
Lanae's Casket – built by close friends of
Logan & Lanae

The casket was built between
April 18th and April 24th ,2022.

"For the mountains may be removed and the
hills may shake
But My lovingkindness will not be removed
from you,
And My covenant of peace will not be
shaken,"
Says the LORD who has compassion on you.
Isaiah 54:10

Message by Judd Lee

First of all, I would like to preface this experience in this way—Lanea was an inspiring individual. She was a friend. She was a sister. Right now, I'm standing in a place where Lanea and I had some very interesting conversations about life and storms and mountains and we were involved in an experience together that kind of built our relationship as friends. Knowing her heart for God and knowing her heart for the oppressed was one of the things that kept me wanting to be close friends with her. So obviously when she passed away, it was a shock to me and I needed to process it.

I found out about what happened to Lanea, while working on a timber-frame structure in Canmore, Alberta. There were

174

some interesting connections to that house I was building. I didn't know who the homeowner was at the time.

That day a stranger visited the construction site. I was processing the news that my friend Rem had shared with me over the phone. This man looked at me standing there looking at some timbers that were supposed to go up into the ceiling. This man approached me and asked me how it was going.

I said "Not great right now for me," and he asked, "Oh, what's going on?"

He didn't tell me who he was.

He just looked at me and I thought, *He's a really happy person. He's joyous and smiling. Why is this guy showing so much interest in how I'm doing? Okay, I'm just going to let him have it.*

So I shared that I was in shock—I had just lost a good friend. She had been in a ski mountaineering accident.

He asked if it was a girl….

"Yeah," I said.

Then he guessed her age and I said, "Yup".

Then he asked if she was John Paetkau's daughter.

I thought, okay, now this is really weird because as a carpenter, on a construction site—to have a stranger come onto the property that you don't know, never mind not knowing that it's the homeowner—to then all of a sudden have a connection to a friend who had just passed away, was just absolutely bizarre.

He said he was really sorry—that he knew John and Leanne—that he knew that Lanea was a really special girl. So, it was really comforting for me to have him there at that moment, knowing I was building a house for somebody that had a connection through missionary work in Ukraine.

I didn't expect what was going to be asked of me next—Lanea's death was still just really fresh news. I don't know how many days after—it could have been three or four maybe five days, I received a phone call from Logan, Lanea's husband. I can't even remember how he posed the question but it was asked in such a way that there was no pressure. Really it was more of a request of, "Judd, would you consider building Lanea's casket for her?"

As a carpenter that's built many things: fences, cabinets, timber frame homes, barns, tables, whatever—lots of different things—I had never, ever before, been asked to build something that had such a substantial human emotional connection—asked to build a friend's casket. So my answer was an overwhelming yes—but that answer came with trepidation and a sense that this needs to be something that honours who she is.

So in that conversation with Logan, I said, "OK well what do you want this to look like?"

He gave me a few things to think about and consider.

"Well, it could have this and if it could have that and could it have this and if you could do that then that would be really great. So I took all of the "if-it-coulds" and made sure these things would all happen.

If I've learned one thing about building something, it's this—it's better to build things with somebody else—in a team. I gathered up the information of the things Logan requested, and shared the details with a lot of my close friends—brothers in Christ who are all carpenters. The group of us gathered together two days after being given the assignment of building Lanea's casket and we went through a very meaningful process over the span of a few days. There was a deadline we had to meet and so it wasn't a lot of time but we knew we had to have it done.

We drove into Calgary, my friend Brayden and I, and picked up all the materials we needed. There were things that were actually being harvested in the bushes such as live poplar branches, because the casket's handles were to be made from those. The pine top was chosen because of Lanea's connection to pine trees. We made sure that there was a living edge pine top. As we were processing how she passed, how she went on to heaven, Brayden found a specific verse that was inscribed on the inside bottom of Lanea's casket.

I was given a task where the attention to detail mattered. I wanted to include everything Logan requested. When you've been given something to do like that, and you want to honour somebody's request in a house it's like, "Oh well the window needs to be over that way a little bit more and that has to be over there and the trim needs to be like this and can you take all this new construction and do your best to do what you can?"

When the carpentry piece is connected to a person in this way, it's very different. I have never experienced something so powerful as a carpenter ever before—to be connected and honoured with the task of building something so special for such a beloved woman.

The different men that came into that experience are all very beautiful, soft, gentle, humble men—carpenters. I could have called upon lots of other friends who are carpenters, but these men were specifically selected because I knew that they would understand the delicacy of this experience. They did.

As I flip through the photos and I see the details—like these butterfly pieces that are here and here and here and…those pieces don't just come together. They have very complex angles and they're designed to lock together into two separate pieces of wood without using screws or fasteners. I watched men putting heart, tender love and care into masterfully creating something beautiful. Sean built those pieces and it was like I was observing his heart going into those pieces. I could see his process of remembering Lanea. We had spent special times together in the same place where we are today.

Someone here—I'm not going to name him, to honour this man—also lost his daughter. Knowing I could call upon him and there would be a different connection for him in this process was another piece to that puzzle. He knew how to honour her. It was so special.

As we record this right now, at this very moment, I am standing beside Lanea's father, John. We are looking at the image of that inscription on my phone together with a friend Robin. We can see right now, visually, the process of the casket being built, through my photos. I am somebody that takes pictures of life. I take pictures of everything. I have a pretty large cloud space and I feel like there's power in imagery and there's power in telling a story. I'm honoured again to be asked to tell a story and I really hope that the readers of this book can grasp what a powerful and profound experience this was for me as a dear friend of Lanea's, but also for all of the other men that came together to build her casket.

The casket was finished April 24th at approximately 2:00 o'clock in the morning. There were a few times (and some people would say it's sleep deprivation... I would argue that there was something else going on) when we had routers, sanders, circular saws, table saws and other tools all going at the same time with all these men together in the room—and this is going to sound weird I think—but I heard an orchestra. I heard music playing with how the different tools were in harmony with one another (I don't even know music-language).

It seemed like God was saying, "Good work guys! Keep going!"
It was so powerful. It was amazing how it all came together.

Then, of course—because I was the one who was asked to put this together—I wasn't 100% sure I wanted to see her in it. I did end up viewing Lanea in her casket. The casket and the flowers—specifically for me the sunflowers—represented her so much.

I was glad to be a part of a process where people felt like she was being honoured. I am thankful I played a small part in shaping the casket and overseeing how it was built—but it was a team of men that came together to do it.

People kept saying, "Great job, great job" to me—but it wasn't just me. It was all of us. It was a group. I was just given the responsibility to make sure it happened. So I think that this was important to share and pass on to people, because they saw that all of those men put so much time and attention and detail into it being what it was.

Preparing for Lanae's burial: Leanne's Story

The day came when we were told the casket was ready to be picked up at David and Mandie Schuler's acreage. I dreaded going there. It was dusk, and I wondered if I would have the strength to go inside the Schuler's shop. I walked in, and there it was on the wooden work horses. It took my breath away. It was so beautiful. So well done.

Logan, John, and Garrett loaded it up into our van, and we left, driving in the dark back to Cochrane. The next day when I got up for work, the shock hit me all over again. There was our van, parked in front of our house, and through the tinted windows I could see the beautiful pine casket that was to be used to bury my daughter. How can this be? How can my daughter's casket be parked, waiting outside of our home? Less than two weeks ago, her car sat parked here, in the same spot, waiting to take her skiing. Life is strange, and death is so wrong.

Logan said he would grab a piece of foam and cut it to fit inside the bottom of the casket. We wanted to give her padding. I realised that we would need to cover that with a sheet—white of course. This is how my mind worked that morning.

Quick, I thought. *Grab my largest white sheet out of our linen closet. That will do. It doesn't matter that it's not freshly washed. A pillow—she will need a pillow to support her neck. I know; the cream/striped brown and green small one from our living room. That will be sufficient. Oh—and a pillow case. Do I have a clean, pretty white one in the closet? Yes, the white with pink and green hand-embroidered one that Siepie gave me years ago from our missionary box at the Bow Island Evangelical Free Church. Wait, something is still missing. Lanae would have rather laid on a bed of Evergreen branches. John can cut some down from behind our house and he and Daniel can bring them along to the funeral home. One more thing. On my way to work that day, I walked and saw baby pine cones—warm brown colours—laying on the pavement. I will come back later and collect quite a few of those. They can be placed around her head, on the branches. That will complete the soft look of the bed that she will lay on as she "sleeps".*

No mother should ever have to gather all the things needed to bury a child of her heart. Death is just so wrong, and God agrees. That's why He sent His Son, His only child to pay the debt for the whole world, to die in our place, and rise again, alive, so that we could live forever, and be truly alive. We must receive His provision for our salvation—to be forever free from death and the curse. If only everyone would choose Him. He is a true Gentleman, and He waits, offering life to everyone.

The funeral director was told the casket would be handmade. They specified the measurements and that it had to be accurate and the handles had to be secure. It needed to fit into a concrete sleeve. The funeral staff were surprised when they saw the casket. The owner of the funeral home commented that he had never seen one so well done.

The family would like to thank the following special people for your labour of love…
all volunteers with Freedom 8848.

Gordon Judson Lee—Master Carpenter
Jerimie Dohnal—Finishing Carpenter
Joe Schellenberg—General Carpenter
Daniel Buhler—Pilot— Carpenter
Andreas Giesbrecht—Pilot
Rembrandt Vlasblom—Pilot;
Coordinator of Freedom 8848
Shawn Rothery—Cabinet maker
Braden Pole—Finishing Carpenter
Unnamed Carpenter (wishes to remain anonymous)
*Built in the shop of David and Mandie Schuler

WHAT IS FREEDOM 8848?

Imagine a groundswell of people standing together, moving mountains for justice

The purpose of Freedom8848 is to support and protect those caught up in the sex trafficking industry. "Sex trafficking seems like a mountain of injustice that cannot be conquered, however, like Mount Everest at 8848 metres, it can be conquered one step at a time.

As ordinary people we can all do our part to help move this mountain, step by step, with becoming informed, challenging social norms, and supporting those in the fight. We believe that hope, restoration, and a bright future can be a reality for anyone."

But to as many as did receive and welcome Him,
He gave the right [the authority, the privilege]
to become children of God, that is, to those
who believe in (adhere to, trust in, and rely
on) His name—
John 1:12

Chapter Ten

Last Steps

Dear Precious Reader,

DEATH IS NOT THE END. IT IS THE BEGINNING. He has prepared a place for us. It is our true home. If we have confessed that Jesus Christ IS Lord, and believed in our heart, that God raised Him from the dead after He was crucified and died for us, FOR OUR SIN!..... one day we will go HOME. We really have no idea, no comprehension, no ability to really imagine what God has in store for those who love Him. It would be like someone trying to explain the world to a baby that hasn't been born. It would be unexplainable.

Where is Lanae? She is not here. Not in Cochrane, not in Blind Bay, you won't find her in Crowsnest Bible Camp—nor in Sumy, Ukraine. Nor is she tramping through the mountain passes—the heights of Yoho National Park—scaling, reaching. Nor skiing—wind flying past, down the powdered backcountry slopes. She is not here right now. Can I take a message? Later she will return your call. She's busy right now—travelling on a trip—an adventure—to a place where she is amazed constantly—overcome by smiles, hugs, music, and celebration. She is in the vestibule—the foyer—the outer hall—in the presence of the groom—waiting for the wedding feast of the Lamb to begin. Who are the guests? All who have accepted God's free invitation and have been adopted into His forever family.

God's plans for Lanae are not finished—the chapters of her forever book are not done. Many previews and trailers have been given to us in God's living Word. I will hear that precious voice once again:

"Hi Mom! MOM! I can't wait to show you… Oh! You'll never guess who I met… MOM IT'S SO COOL!"…and off we will run together…and I at last will keep up.

If you are a praying person reading this right now, please pray that I and many others who are grieving tragedies—big losses—will be able to heal from our grief, our pain, our confusion, and of our distrust, and any unforgiveness we have in our hearts—that we will bundle up these painful emotions and place them in God's loving care. Please pray we will receive joy, healing, forgiveness, freedom, peace, and renewal. Jesus said whatever we loose on Earth will be loosed in Heaven. May we cut the pain loose… and not retain the tragedy as something belonging to us—or we belonging to it.

If you have not yet put your trust in Jesus Christ so you can be saved from eternal death, and eternity in hell (which was made for Satan and the fallen angels, not for you) you can do that today.

Can you see any reason to not give your life to Jesus right now?

"And it shall be that everyone who calls upon the name of the Lord (invoking, adoring, and worshipping the Lord Jesus) shall be saved (rescued spiritually)" Acts 2:21.

"because if you acknowledge and confess with your mouth that Jesus is Lord (recognizing His power, authority, and majesty as God), and believe in your heart that God raised Him from the dead, you will be saved. For with the heart a person believes (in Christ as Saviour) resulting in his justification (that is, being made righteous—being freed of the guilt of sin and made acceptable to God); and with the mouth he acknowledges and confesses (his faith openly), resulting in and confirming (his) salvation." Romans 10:9-10

Please let me know if you have called on Jesus to be your Saviour for the first time, or renewed your desire to follow Him. I would love to direct you as to what the next steps would be, so that you are placed in fertile ground, to grow in your new relationship with God, your Heavenly Father, through Jesus His Son, by the power and strength of the Holy Spirit.

...from Lanae's Journal

February 3, 2020 "Daddy I worship You that You are the Mighty One! You are on my side! You are fighting for me! Thanks for how You took me from fear, feeling discouraged and doubtful to looking forward with GREAT EXPECTATION AND GREAT APPRECIATION for what You have for me! Daddy, what are my steps?"

July 21, 2021 "Jesus, You love to answer my prayers!"

This painting "First Day in Heaven" by Kerolas Safwat, an Egyptian Christian, perfectly captures what Lanae would have done the moment she stepped into glory. No, it isn't a painting of Lanae – it is actually inspired by a photo taken of a Canadian women's soccer team member celebrating a win. But it sure looks like her, doesn't it? As the hymn writer penned "Oh the joy to see my Saviour's face." –John Paetkau

"...and He will wipe away every tear from their eyes;
and there will no longer be death;
there will no longer be sorrow and anguish, or crying, or pain;
for the former order of things has passed away."
Revelation 21:4

198

Epilogue

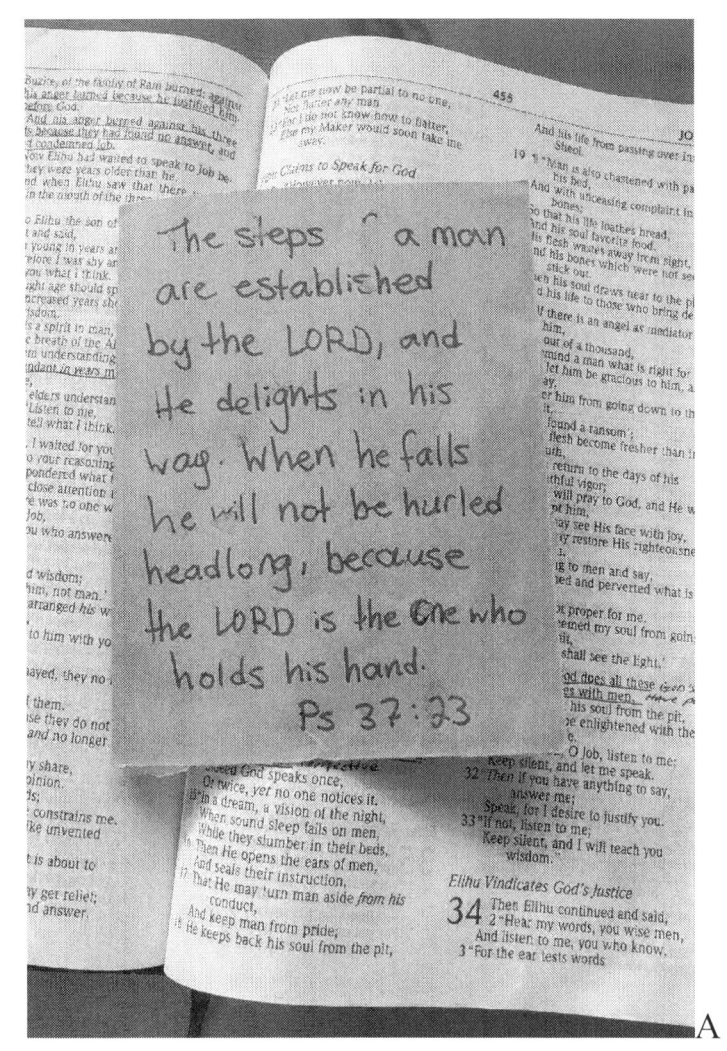

Verse that Lanae gave me (John) a few years
ago with a personal note

Thank you for taking the time to read this book – primarily a glimpse into Leanne's journal as she is walking this path. Our journey through grief has been challenging and continues to be so.

The question is, where do we go from here? Life does go on and each day we have choices that we have to make. Each day we continue to have a sense of loss, a sense of grief, and a sense of just missing Lanae.

These are times that we have been faced as never before with the decision – do we believe what we say we believe? For if we do, then we must choose to act on that belief as we face the inevitable waves of emotion and pain.

Therefore, we choose to trust the truth that we know from God's Word, and to act upon that truth.

In John 14:1 Jesus said to the disciples "Do not let your hearts be troubled; believe in God, believe also in Me." We had to choose to not let our hearts be troubled. We had many questions of "why.....why now? Why her? Why us? why didn't God.....?" Many questions that we won't have the answer for this side of heaven, and ultimately may never be answered. As I wrote earlier, I feel a lot like Job. When we read his story in the Bible, he had a lot of questions and when God answered, God didn't answer Job's questions. What God did was remind Job of who God is and gave Job a bigger perspective. Similar to when I walk down the street with my two year old grandson holding my hand. He isn't concerned with what is two blocks ahead of us, he is enjoying what is nearby, trusting that I am watching what is coming ahead. So, we trust God as we go forward.

Therefore, we choose to continue to be thankful

1 Thessalonians 5:18 says *"in every situation (no matter what the circumstances) be thankful and continually give thanks to God; for this is the will of God for you in Christ Jesus."*

We trust God and His Word, so we continue to choose to look for what we can be thankful for.

We are thankful that Lanae was wearing tech gear (a very good watch) which tracked her GPS, heart rate etc. It survived her fall unscathed, and the data was able to show us exactly what happened. Lanae didn't panic and she didn't suffer for hours awaiting rescue at the foot of the mountain. When we told her sister Alicia the news, Alicia said she knew what Lanae would have done. "The first second her brain would have told her she was falling, the second thought would have been I am going to die, and then she would have started praying for us all." Her heart rate showed a similar progression from exercise rate to brief adrenalin spike, back to exercise rate, to resting. She passed away calmly within 10 minutes from the beginning of the accident.

We are thankful for the Body of Christ, and the outpouring of care from those nearby and from far away. In so many ways we felt the love of God through His children. Messages, food, funds, people dropping by and the list goes on. We were overwhelmed by the care we felt and received.

We are thankful that we KNOW where Lanae is. Many times over the years we as a family would be travelling, and we would agree to meet at a train station, a bus stop or location when we had split up for a time. In essence, Lanae took the early train and she will be waiting for us on the platform when we arrive. What a joyous reunion that will be!

We are thankful that Lanae has begun to experience that which we long for, to be in the presence of Jesus and that which He has prepared for us. There is so much coming, and she already has a glimpse. She is waiting to share so much with us.

We are thankful that we have each new day before us. Every day is an opportunity to grow in our relationship with Jesus, to grow in our relationships with others, and to be used by Christ to make and have an impact in other's lives for eternity. Of course, some days are better than others, but each day is fresh and full of potential.

Therefore, we choose to finish well.

We all are only five steps from eternity. Each day is a gift from God – God Who is the Creator and Sustainer of all things.

It is not an easy path, for this wound of grief will not ever completely heal this side of heaven. We continue to feel sadness, loss, pain, anger and the empty place in our family circle where Lanae stood. We remember all of what we loved in Lanae, and we remember what irritated us too. She wasn't perfect, she is just like all of us—a fallible human being who was in the process of growing, changing, and maturing. But each day is one day closer to our reunion, and therefore we move forward grieving deeply and rejoicing greatly. We have hope for the future, for our hope is firm in Christ Jesus.

John (Lanae's dad) on behalf of Leanne, Logan, Alicia, Garrett & Daniel

*Lanae's Celebration of Life, eulogy etc is posted at thepaetkaus.net/lanea-schroeder-nee-paetkau-1994-2022/

About the Author

Leanne Paetkau lives in Cochrane, Alberta, Canada, with her husband John. They have three adult children, Lanae (who lives in Heaven), Alicia who is married to Garrett Jones (and their children, Liam and Levi), Daniel, and their cat Calvin. Leanne is a graduate of Briercrest College and Seminary in Caronport, Saskatchewan. She and her husband John serve with SEND International of Canada and lived in Ukraine for seventeen years as overseas missionaries.

Follow/Contact Leanne:
www.thepaetkaus.net
Facebook: Leanne Paetkau
Instagram: leannes_place
Email: leanne@thepaetkaus.net

Manufactured by Amazon.ca
Bolton, ON

32547464R00122